WHAT ARE THEY SAYING ABOUT
PAPAL PRIMACY?

What Are They Saying About Papal Primacy?

J. Michael Miller, C.S.B.

PAULIST PRESS
New York/Ramsey

Acknowledgement

The Publisher gratefully acknowledges the use of the following materials: Excerpts from *Papal Primacy and the Universal Church* edited by Paul C. Empie and T. Austin Murphy, © 1974, by permission of Augsburg Publishing House; excerpts from *The Final Report (1982)*, North American Edition, co-published by Forward Movement Publications, 412 Sycamore St., Cincinnati, Ohio 45202 and Office of Publishing Services, U.S. Catholic Conference, 1312 Massachusetts Avenue, NW, Washington, D.C. 20005; excerpts from *The Final Report (1982)*, British Edition, are used also with permission from SPCK (The Society for Promoting Christian Knowledge), and the Catholic Truth Society, London.

Nihil Obstat:
Reverend Monsignor Teodoro de la Torre, S.T.D., Ph.D.
Censor deputatus

Imprimatur:
Most Reverend John L. Morkovsky, S.T.D.
Bishop of Galveston-Houston

July 1, 1982

The *Nihil Obstat* and *Imprimatur* are official declarations that a book or pamphlet is free of doctrinal or moral error. No implication is contained therein that those who have granted the *Nihil Obstat* and *Imprimatur* agree with the contents, opinions or statements expressed.

Library of Congress
Catalog Card Number: 82-60751

ISBN: 0-8091-2501-3

Published by Paulist Press
545 Island Road, Ramsey, N.J. 07446

Printed and bound in the
United States of America

Contents

69863

Preface

Despite the gloomy predictions in the 1970s that the papacy was an ailing, if not dying, institution, the Pope has emerged as a center-stage figure in world and Church affairs in a way which would have been unthinkable twenty years ago. Among Christians of different ecclesial traditions, interest in this ministerial office unique to the Catholic Church is, so to speak, at an all-time high. The death of Paul VI, who guided the Church through the turbulent years after the Second Vatican Council, the brief but sunny pontificate of John Paul I and the immense personal popularity and charisma of John Paul II have all focused our attention on this most ancient of institutions. This book, however, is neither another panegyric nor a critical analysis of these pontificates. Instead, I wish to consider the important, if less known, ecumenical interest in the theology of papal primacy that has been developing since Vatican II.

In recent years certain questions on the papacy have caught the public eye. In light of Hans Küng's book, *Infallible?*[1] and the furor it caused, the dogma of papal infallibility has been examined at length. Here we are not concerned with this particular dimension of the Pope's teaching authority. Rather, we are interested in a prior question: To what extent do Christians agree on the origin and need for a Petrine ministry in the Church? In other words, this is a progress report on what theologians engaged in ecumenical discussions on papal primacy, as well as the official interchurch dialogues themselves, are saying about the following issues: the papacy as a "divine" institu-

1

tion related to Peter's ministry in the apostolic Church, the Pope as a legitimate holder of this Petrine ministry inherited from the apostle, and the papacy as a necessary office of unity at the service of the universal Church.

Using the theological terminology of traditional polemical arguments, briefly outlined in Chapter 1 as background to contemporary discussion, we shall consider the Catholic claim that papal primacy, that is, the task of the bishop of Rome to pastor the universal Church, exists by divine right (*iure divino*) or divine institution (*ex institutione divina*).[2] Is such a claim still an obstacle to the reunion of the churches? What are Catholic, Lutheran and Anglican theologians and interchurch dialogues now saying about the classic Catholic understanding of the divine institution and irrevocable necessity of the papal office?

In the early stages of ecumenical dialogue after Vatican II, the question of papal primacy was studiously avoided. When in 1967 Paul VI commented to the members of the Vatican Secretariat for Promoting Christian Unity that "the Pope . . . is without doubt the most serious obstacle on the road to ecumenism," he articulated a difficulty of which all ecumenists were painfully aware. The implicit taboo against broaching the question of the papacy and its divine right claims has, however, been lifted in recent ecumenical theology.

Discussion and official dialogue are limited in this book to that among Catholics, Lutherans and Anglicans for two reasons. First, each of these churches shares the inheritance of the West with its particular way of looking at the papacy. Thus, the Eastern tradition of Orthodox Christianity is not dealt with. Second, major ecumenical statements have resulted from bilateral dialogues between Catholics and Lutherans, and between Catholics and Anglicans. In the United States, the Lutheran-Catholic Dialogue published a lengthy report, *Differing Attitudes Toward Papal Primacy* (1974), which both summarized and stimulated debate on the papacy. At the international level, the Anglican-Roman Catholic International Commission (AR-CIC), whose Anglican members were appointed by the archbishop of Canterbury and whose Catholic members were appointed by the Vatican's Secretariat for Promoting Christian Unity, has published two agreed statements: *Authority in the Church I* (1976) and *Authority in the Church II* (1981). Although none of these declarations represents the official positions of the churches involved, they are reliable indicators of the progress which theologians and churchmen have made in putting aside bitter polemics. The disputed question of the papacy has been hoisted to a new plane of discourse. In many ways, as we shall see, the old terminology, charged with the overtones of past and present controversy, has dropped away. New ways have opened up.

Ecumenism is a serious concern of the Church as it prepares to enter its third millennium. In an address to the Roman curia on June 28, 1980, John Paul II pointed out the importance of ecumenism as "a priority imposed on our actions, in the first place because it corresponds to the very vocation of the Church. The ecumenical effort is not engaged in for reasons of opportuneness and is not dictated by contingent situations or circumstances, but is based on God's will." Such is our mandate. This book will therefore fulfill its purpose if it succeeds in demonstrating that among Catholics, Lutherans and Anglicans a growing convergence of opinion on the origin and necessity of the papacy is emerging. Though not all the theological difficulties on papal primacy have been removed, the mainline views on the papacy as expressed by each tradition are now closer than at any time since the separation of the churches in the sixteenth century. To recognize and welcome such progress is cause for renewed hope about the role of papal ministry in a reunited Church of the third millennium.

Notes

1. (Garden City, 1971).
2. For a thorough historical and doctrinal treatment of the papacy as an institution of divine right, see J. Michael Miller, *The Divine Right of the Papacy in Recent Ecumenical Theology,* Analecta Gregoriana, 218 (Rome, 1980).

1
Our Roots: Polemical Traditions

Catholics, Lutherans and Anglicans all have a traditional and well-defined teaching on papal primacy. The contemporary dialogue on the papacy comes into focus, however, only after a look at the roots of each ecclesial tradition. Thus, we must first consider where we have come from and how each group has reached its present understanding. Such an examination will then help us to appreciate questions raised and advances made through ecumenical dialogue.

Catholics

Leonine Tradition

Theologians agree that Pope Leo I (†461) drew together the threads of the earlier patristic theology of papal primacy which had been in the process of formation, especially in the West, for at least two centuries. Leo summed up this Roman tradition by clearly explaining the relationship between Christ and Peter, and between Peter and the bishop of Rome. His views largely determined the Latin West's understanding of the theological foundation for the papacy.

Leo's appeal to the Petrine text of Mt 16:18–19 ("You are Peter and upon this rock I will build my church . . .") as justification for his office followed in the tradition of Pope Stephen I (†257) who had already invoked the Matthew text to justify papal authority. Leo, however, emphasized forcefully that Christ himself gave to Peter personally, and to him alone, a primatial role in the apostolic college. Peter's authority over the apostles was a sharing in the sacred authority or *potestas* of Christ (Sermon 3.3).[1] Between Jesus and Peter so intimate a relationship existed that the apostle's judgments were considered to be identical with those of Christ (Sermon 3.4). Thus, Leo argued, Peter had received a "primacy" in the apostolic college by dominical institution, that is, from Christ the Lord himself.

In addition to his insistence that Jesus gave to Peter a primacy over the other apostles, Leo held that the Pope continued to fulfill Peter's role in the Church. Although the idea of the Roman bishop as successor to Peter was already known in the ecclesiastical tradition at Rome, such papal assertions were isolated (DS 181). But Leo had been trained in Roman law and explained his understanding of papal succession through use of the legal concept of heredity. In the tradition of Roman law familiar to him, the heir was acknowledged as having the same rights, authority and obligations as the one he replaced.[2] In like manner, then, the Pope could exercise the same office and fullness of authority that Christ had entrusted to Peter. After the death of Peter, the Pope was both his successor in the historical sense and his substitute or vicar in the legal sense.

Further, according to Leo, Peter continued to exercise authority in the Church in a mystical way. This mystical identification of the heir with the deceased was not found in Roman law. To the idea of juridical continuity through succession in office Leo added that of mystical or sacramental continuity: from heaven Peter continues to pray for the Church and to govern it through his heir and vicar, the bishop of Rome (Sermon 3.2). In this sense *Papa = Petrus ipse*; the Pope is Peter himself. Leo founded the permanence of the papacy on Peter's unfailing guidance of the Church. Therefore, Christ not only instituted Petrine primacy but also continues to guide the Church through a living Petrine authority. Consequently, papal primacy itself is also willed by Christ.

When the Eastern representatives drew up canon 28 at the Council of Chalcedon (451) without the participation of the papal legates, they affirmed that "to the throne of Old Rome, the Fathers gave privileges with good reason, because it was the imperial city." Leo interpreted this canon as a denial of the divine institution of papal primacy, since it based the bishop of Rome's first place in the

Church merely on the city's political status as the capital of the Empire. Roman primacy would, then, appear to be simply a matter of historical and ecclesiastical arrangement. Although it is now debated whether in fact the canon did deny the divine right claims of the Roman See, Leo refused to ratify the canon, basing his objection on the Council Fathers' reliance on political grounds alone as the basis for primatial authority. In any case, Leo seized the opportunity to clarify a fundamental doctrinal issue: the bishop of Rome succeeded to Peter's role in the Church because of Christ's will, not because of a conciliar decision or a political reason. Papal primacy, he held, was of divine, and not of ecclesiastical institution.

Right up until the present day Leo's teaching on the dominical institution of the papacy has dominated Catholic theology. Church councils in the Middle Ages incorporated into their official teachings the Leonine view on the origin of papal primacy. At the Second Council of Lyons (1274) the profession of faith of Michael Paleologus affirmed that the church at Rome had full and supreme authority over the universal Church and that this had been granted "by the Lord himself in blessed Peter, prince or head of the apostles" (DS 861). The Council of Florence (1439) repeated this affirmation with reference to the Pope: "To him in blessed Peter was given by our Lord Jesus Christ the full power of feeding, ruling and governing the universal Church" (DS 1307). Both councils upheld the view which prevailed in the Middle Ages: the primacy of Peter, and consequently of the Pope, "in blessed Peter," was conferred by Christ himself and continued to exist as an institution which Jesus himself had established in the Church.

During the sixteenth century the reformers raised the question of the right by which the Pope exercised his authority over the universal Church. In reply to Martin Luther's rejection of papal primacy, Catholics restated and clarified their teaching on the papacy. Cajetan, for example, defended the divine right of papal primacy in *The Divine Institution of the Pontifical Office over the Whole Church in the Person of the Apostle Peter* (1521), a systematic defense of the Catholic position. He bequeathed to later theology an apologetical framework which distinguished three questions to be dealt with: (1) Peter's primacy in the apostolic college (Petrine primacy); (2) the successor to Peter's ministry (Petrine succession); (3) the bishop of

Rome as the legitimate successor to Peter. In spite of the Protestant reformers' denial of Roman authority, however, the Council of Trent did not issue any pronouncement on papal primacy. Like all Catholics at the time, the Council Fathers clearly held to the Leonine and medieval understanding of the papacy, an understanding which post-Tridentine theologians taught right up to its incorporation into the dogmatic definitions of the First Vatican Council in 1870.

Vatican I and Afterward

The definition of papal primacy in Vatican I's document *Pastor Aeternus* adds nothing doctrinally to the teaching of Leo the Great as it was handed on in the Church after the Council of Trent. The Council Fathers at Vatican I dealt explicitly in Chapter 1 with the institution of Petrine primacy and in Chapter 2 with the perpetuity of this primacy in the Roman Pontiff.

1. Petrine Primacy

The opening sentence of Chapter 1 of *Pastor Aeternus* is the Council's solemn and authoritative reaffirmation of the Catholic tradition on the dominical institution of Petrine primacy: "We teach and declare therefore, that according to the testimony of the Gospel, a primacy of jurisdiction over the whole Church of God has been promised and conferred immediately and directly on blessed Peter by Christ the Lord" (DS 3053). The Fathers asserted that Christ has constituted Peter head of the apostolic college and that this was the teaching of Scripture "as it had always been understood by the Catholic Church" (DS 3054). They invoked three texts—Jn 1:42, Mt 16:18–19 and Jn 21:15–17—to prove that Christ himself had promised and handed over to Peter alone a primacy of jurisdiction (DS 3053). Using the standard interpretation of the Petrine texts which had prevailed in Catholic theology since Leo the Great, Vatican I taught that Jesus himself had given to Peter a primacy of jurisdiction over the whole Church.

2. Petrine Succession

Chapter 2 of *Pastor Aeternus* deals with Petrine succession and states that what Christ established in the person of blessed Peter for the good of the Church belongs to it permanently (DS 3056). The canon attached to the chapter anathematizes anyone who denies that it is "according to the institution of Christ our Lord himself, that is, by divine right, that St. Peter has perpetual successors in the primacy over the whole Church" (DS 3058). Thus, Christ instituted successors to Peter, not just the first Pope.

The deliberations of the Preparatory Theological Commission of Vatican I give no hint that these theologians considered any other justification for the papacy than that of dominical institution. Its members wanted the Council Fathers to condemn as heretics those who thought the development of papal primacy was due to ecclesiastical law or to the imperial importance of Rome. Following the theologians' recommendations, the Council Fathers deliberately excluded the opinion of those who denied the divine institution of papal primacy.

On the other hand, in spite of some pressure to do so, the Fathers did not define that the bishop of Rome, rather than the bishop of any other see, was the successor to Peter by divine right. They merely affirmed the *de facto* situation: the Roman Pontiff is to be considered as the legitimate heir of Peter's primacy over the Church.

However, the modernists, a group of Catholic dissidents in the early twentieth century, provoked Catholic apologists to insist once again on the divine institution of papal primacy (DS 3455–3456). Pius X's official reaffirmation of the dominical origin of the papacy became the commonplace view presented in pre-Vatican II theology. Papal primacy has been taught in recent years, therefore, to be of divine right and not of human (apostolic or ecclesiastical) right.

Prior to Vatican II, nearly every twentieth-century theology of the papacy adopted the manner of presentation and definitions of *Pastor Aeternus:* (1) Petrine primacy promised and conferred by Christ; (2) the perpetuity of succession in the primacy; and (3) the legitimacy of the bishop of Rome's claim to be the successor of Peter. One would look in vain in the classic manuals of theology and canon law for any dissent regarding the dominical institution of either Petrine primacy or Petrine succession, the twin pillars which provided the papacy with its theological justification to be an institution of divine right.

To hold that papal primacy was of divine right was more than an affirmation of its dominical origin. It also involved certain consequences for the present and for the future. Theologians considered the papacy to belong to the permanent constitution of the Church as an absolutely necessary element of its hierarchical structure. This radical immutability was based on a universally accepted assumption: what Christ had instituted was of its very nature unchangeable. No Catholic ever suggested that an institution of divine right, such as the papacy, was either transitory or reversible.

Lutherans

Martin Luther, Philip Melanchthon, and other sixteenth-century reformers formulated a position which rejected traditional Catholic teaching on the divine institution of the papacy. This polemical stance determined the negative Lutheran attitude to papal primacy until the mid-twentieth century. At the same time, however, this classical tradition allowed for a kind of conditional acceptance of the papacy.

Rejection of Papal Primacy

Just when Luther began to propose unorthodox views on the papacy is a moot point. It is clear, however, that in his 1519 dispute at Leipzig with John Eck, an ardent upholder of the traditional Roman claims, Luther denied the divine institution of papal primacy. From the outset Eck realized the significance of Luther's denial. To this end, the Roman apologist reiterated the traditional Catholic teaching that there was no papal primacy without Petrine primacy and no Petrine primacy if Christ had not addressed to Peter, as the first Pope, the words which Scripture recorded in the Gospels of Matthew and John.

Luther formulated his response in terms of his critics' arguments. Other reformers, including Melanchthon, adopted a similar method. They systematically challenged the theological justification for papal primacy which had been widely accepted in the Western Church.

Luther was keenly aware of the importance of Mt 16:18–19 to a theology of the papacy. Following the interpretation of some early

Church Fathers, Luther did not consider the "rock" of verse 18 to be the apostle Peter and his successors. Rather, this rock referred to the faith of Peter, the representative of all Christians, upon which the Lord promised to build his Church. The power of the "keys" in verse 19 was not given to Peter alone, but to the whole Church—that is, "neither to Peter nor to a successor, nor to any one church, but to all the churches."[3] Luther thus attacked the two fundamental pillars of traditional belief: Petrine primacy and Petrine succession. According to Luther, Christ neither promised nor gave any primacy in the Church to Peter or to anyone who claimed to be his successor. Furthermore, because Jesus had promised that the gates of hell would not prevail against what was erected on rock, that edifice could not be the historical papacy: "The gates of hell have frequently contained the papacy. . . . God would never have permitted this to happen if, in Christ's words, the rock meant this same papacy. For then his promise would not be true, and he would not fulfill his own words."[4]

Luther's exegesis of Jn 21:15–17 likewise departed from the conventional Western interpretation. The Lord's command to feed his sheep did not confer any primacy upon Peter. In his threefold question to Peter "Do you love me more than these?" Christ demanded an exceptional love of God from those exercising ministry in the Church.[5] Here again Luther pointed to the deficiencies of many Popes. Thus, neither could the Johannine text apply to the papacy.

Melanchthon agreed with his mentor's reading of the Petrine texts. On the basis of Scripture he too denied the existence of a biblical foundation for the primacy of one apostle over any other. The legitimacy of a primatial office such as the papacy was therefore an a priori impossibility. Since Luther and Melanchthon rejected the very existence of Petrine primacy, they treated the question of succession to Peter's position by the Pope as secondary. Nonetheless, to oppose Catholic teaching, the reformers developed their own views on why the papacy did evolve in the early Church.

As early as 1519, Luther's study of the history of the papacy in his *Resolution Concerning the Power of the Pope* persuaded him that the Pope owed his primacy in the Church to human and ecclesiastical law. The Roman church came to enjoy its superior position on account of the decrees of the Roman Pontiffs themselves, decrees which contradicted the teaching of Scripture. Furthermore, conciliar decisions also served to bolster Rome's primatial status in the ancient Church.

Melanchthon's *Treatise on the Power and Primacy of the Pope* (1537) likewise attributed the origin of the papacy to ecclesiastical law. By citing a series of patristic and conciliar texts, Melanchthon attempted to prove that primatial authority was neither exercised nor acknowledged in the ancient Church; consequently, the papacy "was not instituted by Christ and does not come from divine right."[6] According to the reformers' most polemical writings, therefore, the Pope's claim to succeed to a Christ-given primacy bestowed on Peter was without any foundation.

A Reformed Papacy?

In some writing, however, the reformers tempered their rejection of the dominical origin of papal primacy with a willingness to accept some kind of modified papacy. The young Luther was willing to attribute a certain legitimacy to the papacy, even as a "divinely willed" institution. During the controversy over indulgences he recognized that God "ordained" the papacy as he did legitimate secular institutions of authority. Thus, at the outset of his difficulties with Rome Luther did not dissent from the papacy itself but from the theological arguments used to legitimate it. He accepted papal primacy as an historical institution ordained by God and shaped by man. Within the juridical organization of the Christian community the bishop of Rome was above others. If the Pope would submit to the judgment of the word of God and renounce his claim that submission to the papacy was necessary for salvation, then Luther would acknowledge the papacy as a legitimate ecclesial structure of human institution. But if the Pope would not accept this, insisting rather on the divine institution of the papacy, then he was to be considered as the antichrist.[7]

Despite his skepticism about the real possibility of a reformed papacy, Luther was disposed until very late in his career to tolerate Christian unity under a Pope who justified his office only as a human institution. As the years passed, however, Luther changed his mind. In the *Smalcald Articles* of 1537, he wrote: "Manifestly (to repeat what has already been said often) the papacy is a human invention, and it is not commanded, it is unnecessary, and it is useless."[8] By this time Luther had become convinced that the Pope would never renounce the claim that the papacy originated in the will of Christ.

Near the end of his life Luther reproached himself for his earlier, more tolerant views. Now persuaded of the blasphemous nature of the papacy, he repeatedly stressed its demonic origins in his last polemical work, *Against the Roman Papacy, an Institution of the Devil* (1545). This final bitter attitude was the most influential on subsequent generations who attributed to the papacy no legitimacy whatsoever, even as an institution of human right.

Whereas Luther eventually abandoned hope for a reformed papacy, Melanchthon did not. The more conciliatory Melanchthon added his famous subscript to the *Smalcald Articles*: "Concerning the Pope I hold that, if he would allow the Gospel, we, too, may concede him that superiority over the bishops which he possesses by human right, making this concession for the sake of peace and general unity among Christians who are now under him and who may be in the future."[9] In this carefully prepared statement, Melanchthon thus admitted the legitimacy of the papacy only if it is considered an institution of human, not divine, right. Though Melanchthon's conciliatory position appeared in the definitive statement of Lutheran orthodoxy formulated in the *Book of Concord* (1580), most Lutherans of the following generations shaped their views on papal primacy from Luther's later and more anti-papal writings.

Anglicans

Sixteenth-Century Anti-Papal Polemic

The Act of Supremacy of 1534 definitively declared the independence of the English national church from the papacy and provided the occasion for the anti-papal polemic which was widespread in the years following the crown's assumption of control over the Church. As on the continent, theologians began to describe the Pope as the antichrist. The first English Litany of 1544 contained a petition which begged the Lord to deliver the people "from the tyranny of the Bishop of Rome and all his detestable enormities." Article 37 of the Thirty-Nine Articles succinctly denied the papal claims in England: "The Bishop of Rome hath no jurisdiction in this Realm of England." At the outset, the English theologians attacked the abuses of Roman authority, but they soon went on to question the very legitimacy of the papal office itself.

John Jewel (†1571), bishop of Salisbury, served as an official apologist in the formative years of Anglicanism. Like other theologians, he realized that the Petrine function of the papacy was essential to Rome's claim to primacy over the universal Church. Jewel attacked on two counts. First, like the Lutherans, he rejected any biblical basis for the papacy. He denied that Peter had received any authority which distinguished him from the other apostles. The "rock" in Mt 16:18 did not refer to Peter but to Christ: "The old Catholic Fathers have written and pronounced not any mortal man, as Peter was, but Christ himself, the Son of God, to be this rock."[10] He buttressed his interpretation with a long list of anti-Roman patristic texts and concluded that Petrine primacy was not testified to in the Scriptures. Furthermore, Peter received nothing from Christ which set him apart from the other apostles: "These words (Mt 16:18–19), saith he [Origen], are not spoken directly or only unto Peter, but as unto Peter. And the other apostles have the keys and are the rock, as well as Peter."[11] Because of the absence of a biblical witness to its dominical institution, concluded Jewel, papal primacy was not of divine right.

Second, the episcopal apologist argued that Rome's privileged position in the early Church was based on mere secular and historical reasons. Like his view on Petrine primacy, his refutation of the origin of papal primacy became standard in later Anglican apologetics. Jewel did not deny that the bishop of Rome had at one time enjoyed an "estimation, and a credit, and a prerogative before all others."[12] Nonetheless, this prominence was not due to Christ's will. The Pope had acquired this role in the early Church because of the importance of his bishopric: the antiquity of Rome as a see, its preservation of the memory of St. Peter, its numerous martyrs, its orthodox faith, and especially its imperial significance as affirmed in the First Council of Constantinople.[13] From the beginning, then, Anglican theologians admitted that Rome and its bishop enjoyed a certain pre-eminent role in the life of the early Church, even though they did so no longer. But at no time did they ever consider such a function to be dominically mandated.

Papacy Reconsidered: The Caroline Divines

In the seventeenth century, however, Anglican churchmen and theologians acknowledged that Peter's privileges were confirmed in the Scriptures. Because of their historical studies, these Caroline divines did not dispute the glowing tribute which so many of the early Fathers, especially in the West, had paid to St. Peter. Nonetheless, following the opinion of Archbishop William Laud (†1645), they limited these privileges which Jesus conferred on Peter to the apostle alone "in his own person."[14] Isaac Barrow (†1677), in agreeing with Laud's view, asked whether Rome owed its primatial position to Petrine succession, and he answered, "No; that was a slim, upstart device, that did not hold for Antioch, nor in other apostolic Churches."[15] No Anglican at that time entertained the idea that the bishop of Rome personally succeeded to the role Peter had held in the early Church.

Despite their denial of Petrine succession, the Caroline divines nonetheless adopted a more positive view of the development of the historic papacy because of the major institutional role it had played in the patristic Church. They recognized the Pope as patriarch of the West. In *A Relation of the Conference between William Laud and Mr. Fisher the Jesuit,* Archbishop Laud acknowledged that "the Roman patriarch, by ecclesiastical constitutions, might perhaps have a primacy of order—but for the principality of power, the patriarchs were as even, as equal, as the apostles were before them."[16] The church at Rome was the "principal church" of Christendom with a "primacy of order." Admissions of such a Roman primacy abound in the writings of the Caroline divines. Most significantly, they acknowledged that whatever limited role the Pope had played in the ancient Church he could play again, provided that such a primacy was regarded as an institution of only human right.

Lutheran and Anglican opinions on the theological justification for the papacy changed very little from the seventeenth to the twentieth centuries. Along with the polemical anti-papal current of Luther and of the first generation of English reformers co-existed a more tolerant view of the papacy in the writings of Melanchthon and the Caroline divines. Thus, even though in fact all Lutherans and Anglicans rejected the Catholic understanding of papal primacy, at the same time each tradition contains the basis for a positive re-evaluation of this office, an appreciation which the twentieth-century ecumenical movement has been able to exploit.

Notes

1. See the three sermons of Leo I preached on the anniversary of his episcopal ordination in *Nicene and Post-Nicene Fathers,* 2nd series (Grand Rapids, 1956) 12, 115–118.

2. Walter Ullmann, "Leo I and the Theme of Papal Primacy," *Journal of Theological Studies* 11 (1960) 33–35.

3. "Resolutio Lutheriana super propositione sua decima tertia de potestate papae," in *D. Martin Luthers Werke: Kritische Gesamtausgabe* (Weimar, 1883ff) 2, 191.

4. "On the Papacy in Rome, Against the Most Celebrated Romanist in Leipzig," in *Luther's Works,* ed. Eric W. Gritsch (Philadelphia, 1970) 39, 93–94.

5. "Resolutio Lutheriana," 188.

6. *The Book of Concord: The Confessions of the Evangelical Lutheran Church,* ed. Theodore G. Tappert (Philadelphia, 1958) 322–323.

7. "On the Papacy in Rome," 101–102.

8. *Book of Concord,* 299.

9. *Ibid.,* 316–317.

10. *The Works of John Jewel,* ed. John Ayre (Cambridge, 1845) 1, 340.

11. "A Defence of the Apology of the Church of England," *Works of Jewel,* 3, 289.

12. *Works of Jewel,* 1, 375.

13. *Ibid.,* 370.

14. *The Works of William Laud,* ed. William Scott, 6th ed. (Oxford, 1849) 2, 205.

15. *Anglicanism: The Thought and Practice of the Church of England, Illustrated from the Religious Literature of the Seventeenth Century,* ed. Paul Elmer More and Frank Leslie Cross (1935; rpt. London, 1962) 63.

16. *Works of Laud,* 2, 186.

2
Jesus and Peter

Since Vatican II, Catholics, Lutherans, and Anglicans have all launched a determined effort to move beyond the sterile intransigence of the past and to re-evaluate their traditional stances on the origin and necessity of the papacy. At the heart of this re-examination is the question whether Jesus bestowed on Peter any special ministry in the apostolic college which is the basis of papal primacy. Let us now ask what contemporary Catholic, Lutheran and Anglican theologians are saying about the institution of *Petrine* primacy by Jesus Christ.

Catholics

In recent years a number of Catholic theologians have assailed the traditional interpretation of the divine institution of papal primacy with a barrage of arguments contesting its dominical foundation. Historians of the early Church have revealed the formative role of the primitive community in shaping its own ecclesial structures. Scripture scholars, aware of the early community's role in composing the New Testament, have made it increasingly difficult to use the Petrine texts as self-evident proofs that Jesus assigned Peter a special ministry. Theologians, using the findings of both the historians and the Scripture scholars, must again ask: Is it still possible to maintain that Petrine primacy was instituted by the Lord himself?

This question evokes at least two different answers from contemporary Catholic theologians. A minority, whom we can describe as "functionalists," no longer accept that there is any foundation for the papacy in Christ's conferral of a ministry on Peter. The majority, the "scripturalists," still acknowledge a dominical basis for the Pope's ministry to the universal Church as witnessed to in Sacred Scripture.

Functionalists

Some contemporary scholars have raised the question of the immediate and direct institution by Christ of the Church's hierarchical ministry. In his description of the origin of ecclesial office, Edward Schillebeeckx summarizes this recent opinion: "There is no direct link between the contemporary offices of the Church (the episcopate, the presbyterate, and the diaconate) and an act of institution on the part of Jesus while he was on earth."[1] The Church's primatial-episcopal structure did not come ready-made from Christ himself but from a combination of divine and human factors. Both functionalists and scripturalists agree that free human decisions played a role in the development of the Church's constitution, but they differ on the theological value to be attributed to these factors.

Catholic functionalists, such as Hans Küng, Gotthold Hasenhüttl, and Karl-Heinz Ohlig, deny the basis for the papacy in a Petrine "primacy" conferred by Christ. Yet, as Catholic theologians, they must somehow deal with the First Vatican Council's teaching in *Pastor Aeternus* which we examined in Chapter 1. Ohlig, for example, thinks that the Council Fathers made use of the Petrine texts in their pronouncements simply to legitimate a *de facto* development in the Church's structure. He maintains there is no proof that Jesus gave to Peter a primatial role in the early community. Ohlig therefore concludes that the Council Fathers merely affirmed the legitimate existence of the papacy and made no claim regarding its origin in the will of Christ.

Aware of the difficulty in separating Vatican I's affirmation of the Pope as the pinnacle of the Church's hierarchy from the theological justification given to the papacy, Ohlig relies on the distinction between an ecclesiastical and a critical reading of Scripture. An ecclesiastical reading of Scripture is not primarily concerned with the sacred text itself; it focuses, rather, on a contemporary religious issue which the Church explains by using illuminating passages from the Scriptures. When the Fathers invoked the Petrine texts from the Gospel, Ohlig continues, they did not intend to make any exegetical affirmations; that is, they avoided solemnly teaching that Jesus really conferred a ministry on Peter which could be inherited by a successor. By incorporating these traditional texts into *Pastor Aeternus* the Fathers wished only to profess their conviction that the papacy was a legitimate institution not opposed to the New Testament. According to Ohlig, then, Vatican I did not affirm that the Pope succeeded to a ministry instituted by Christ but simply maintained that it was a structure in harmony with God's plan for his Church.[2] Common to the functionalists is their abandoning the traditional Catholic interpretation which holds that the theological justification of the historic papacy is found in the ministry that Jesus assigned to Peter.

Scripturalists

In the first speech of his pontificate on October 17, 1979, Pope John Paul II reiterated the importance of the three traditional Petrine texts (Mt 16:18–19; Lk 22:31–32; Jn 21:15–17) to a Catholic theology of the papacy: "We are completely convinced that all modern inquiry into the 'Petrine ministry' must be based on these three hinges of the Gospel." Similarly most Catholic theologians still stress the Petrine foundation for the papal ministry, a position in keeping with a long tradition of the magisterium and of theology. The Councils of Florence and Vatican I both taught the dominical institution of Petrine primacy as the theological basis for papal primacy. Furthermore, the Fathers at Vatican II had no intention of renouncing the teaching of *Pastor Aeternus* on the papacy: "This teaching concerning the institution, the permanence, the nature and import of the sacred primacy of the Roman Pontiff and his infallible teaching office, the sacred synod proposes anew to be firmly believed by all the faithful" (*Lumen Gentium,* 18). The Council made a point of specifically reaffirming that Peter had received his special commission from Jesus himself: "The Lord made Peter alone the rock-foundation and the holder of the keys of the Church (cf Mt 16:18–19), and constituted him shepherd of his whole flock (cf Jn 21:15–17)" (*Lumen Gentium,* 22).

According to scripturalists like Yves Congar, Avery Dulles, Walter Kasper, Karl Rahner and Leo Scheffczyk, Catholic teaching must continue to link the present primacy of the Pope to the ministry of the apostle Peter. Without some kind of original Petrine primacy, the Catholic claims for the papacy rest on sand. With the exception of a few functionalists, Catholic theologians hold firmly to this traditional understanding. Taking into account the results of contemporary scriptural research, they still affirm a biblical basis for the existence of a Petrine primacy in the apostolic college. To justify the papacy in accordance with the Catholic tradition, they refer to Vatican II's analogy between Peter's role among the apostles in the apostolic college and that of the Pope among the other bishops in the episcopal college: "Just as, in accordance with the Lord's decree, St. Peter and the rest of the apostles constitute a unique apostolic college, so in like fashion the Roman Pontiff, Peter's successor, and the bishops, the successors of the apostles, are related with and united to one another" (*Lumen Gentium,* 22).

Yet, to insist on the significance of the classical Petrine texts for the origin of the papacy is not the same as defending the interpretation given to them by the Fathers at Vatican I. In fact, the Council did not give these texts any authoritative interpretation. Theologians are bound only to the Fathers' conclusions but not to their exegesis. Evaluating the official exegesis proposed by the Theological Commission at Vatican I, Gustave Thils believes that their scriptural argument was a case of special pleading. The official theologians at the Council sought a New Testament foundation for their dogmatic teaching on the papacy. Because it lacked the perspective given by more recent exegesis, this official interpretation is "distressing," and also, according to Thils, contains as much error as truth.[3] Present-day theologians, he says, have sufficient grounds for holding that Peter received a special ministry from Jesus without relying upon Vatican I's dated exegesis of the Petrine texts. Like Thils, nearly all Catholic theologians still maintain that the papacy must in some way be related to the unique share in his authority which Christ himself conferred on Peter.

Lutherans

A very significant ecumenical breakthrough since Vatican II has been the reappraisal of the papacy by Lutherans and Anglicans. Theologians of both these traditions have begun to re-evaluate the question of a possible Petrine primacy justified on the basis of New Testament teaching.

In recent years many Lutherans, led by a group of "revisionist" theologians, including among others Harding Meyer and Wolfhart Pannenberg from Germany and Joseph Burgess and George Lindbeck from the United States, have laid aside the reformers' polemical exegesis of the Petrine texts which led them to undercut the Catholic justification for Petrine primacy. Even before Vatican II, there was a small group of theologians, including Richard Baumann and Hans Asmussen, who accepted that Peter held a unique and privileged position among the other apostles. They were willing to attribute a dominical foundation to this ministry, though they still had difficulty in relating it to the way in which later Popes exercised ecclesial authority.[4] By admitting that Peter was the rock upon whom Christ promised to build the Church, these revisionists acknowledged the existence within the apostolic community of a specific Petrine ministry which originated with the will of Jesus Christ. At first, this so-called "Romanizing tendency" was confined to a small group. With recent interest in ecumenical dialogue, however, other theologians are moving this interpretation into the mainstream of Lutheran exegesis.[5]

Popular adult catechisms such as the recently published catechism of the United Evangelical Lutheran Church of Germany also demonstrate this new openness. This catechism openly rejects the traditional Lutheran view and espouses the more recent biblical exegesis in which Peter himself is the "rock" upon whom Christ promised to build his Church (Mt 16:18).[6] Thus, in some circles at least, the problem to be resolved no longer concerns so much the scriptural basis for a Petrine "primacy" but whether such a primacy was later to continue in the Church.

Not all Lutheran theologians, however, agree that the Petrine texts provide a scriptural basis for any kind of primacy. Wolfhart Pannenberg, for instance, is very open to a possible role for the papacy but he insists that Lutherans not be forced to swallow a Catholic interpretation of a biblically warranted Petrine ministry. He laments the lack of attention paid to the scriptural data which challenge the idea of an exclusive leadership role for Peter. Because of the alleged weakness of the biblical argument, Pannenberg proposes that ecumenists consider the possibility of a divinely-based but non-scriptural justification for papal primacy, one independent of the acceptance of Petrine primacy.[7] Since, as he says, the papacy developed in the early Church without recourse to a Petrine foundation, the contemporary Church can justify the papacy as more than a functional reality without reference to Jesus' conferring a leadership role on Peter. Despite this warning of Pannenberg, many Lutherans who are favorably disposed toward the papacy have laid aside the scriptural exegesis of the sixteenth century and are now approaching the question of Petrine primacy in a new light.

Lutheran-Catholic Dialogue

The conclusions of the American Lutheran-Catholic Dialogue published in *Differing Attitudes Toward Papal Primacy* (1974)[8] mirror the views of both Catholic scripturalists and moderate Lutheran revisionists. Both parties in the Dialogue admit that "it is now clear that the question of papal primacy cannot adequately be treated in terms of proof passages from Scripture" (#14). For their part, the Catholics agree it is anachronistic to insist that Jesus made Peter the first "Pope." Furthermore, they admit that "terms such as 'primacy' and 'jurisdiction' are best avoided when one describes the role of Peter in the New Testament" (#9). In return, the Lutherans concede that they cannot a priori deny to Peter a special leadership role in the apostolic Church. The conclusion which emerges from their discussion is the growing agreement on a New Testament foundation for a Petrine "primacy," a concession made by the Lutherans, but not necessarily agreement on its actual dominical foundation, a concession made by the Catholics. Consequently, the participants of both traditions can now accept Petrine primacy to be "divinely" instituted—a designation which leaves open the question whether this function depends on the will of Jesus or of the apostolic community.

The Catholic members of the American Dialogue questioned their own long-held assumptions about the origins of the papal office.

They do not insist that holding papal primacy to be divinely instituted necessarily implies believing that Christ established it by a formal
act attested to either in Scripture or in the apostolic tradition. Thus,
the Catholic participants conclude that their traditional description
"does not adequately communicate what we believe concerning the
divine institution of the papacy" (#50).

For their part, the Lutheran participants accept that the New
Testament describes Peter as having a leadership role in the apostolic
Church: "Exegetically it is hard to deny that Peter enjoyed a pre-
eminence among the apostles during Jesus' ministry as well as in the
post-Easter Church. He exercised in his time a function on behalf of
the unity of the entire apostolic Church" (#40). In order to justify
this conclusion, the Lutheran members of the American Dialogue
present selected scriptural interpretations from the reformers and
from their classical theologians to demonstrate how the Lutheran
tradition does, in fact, support a certain kind of Petrine primacy
among the apostles (#38). But neither their own sources nor the
participants themselves affirm that Christ conferred this function on
Peter. In this way they differ from the Catholic participants. Nonetheless, both Lutherans and Catholics are moving toward a shared
opinion on a New Testament, if not dominical, foundation for Petrine primacy.

Anglicans

From the seventeenth to the twentieth century, Anglican opinions on the kind of justification which could be given to the papacy
changed very little. As we have already outlined in Chapter 1, two
interpretations surfaced in the Anglican tradition: one which was
strongly anti-papal and another one which was more open to the papacy as an ecclesiastical office. Nowadays it is becoming more common than ever for Anglican theologians to defend the dominical
institution of Petrine primacy.

Relying on the interpretations of the Caroline divines, some
modern Anglican theologians have acknowledged that St. Peter held
the leading position in the apostolic college on the basis of dominical
institution. Already at the Malines Conversations (1921–1925) between Anglicans and Catholics an Anglican participant admitted

that "the evidence of the New Testament justifies us in saying that St. Peter was chosen and marked out by our Lord to exercise a primacy of leadership among the Twelve—to be their spokesman and leader, though not their ruler."[9] A few years later the Anglican Church historian B. J. Kidd maintained that Peter enjoyed a primacy of leadership among the Twelve, though Kidd did not intend thereby to legitimate the present exercise of papal authority.[10] Michael Ramsey, later archbishop of Canterbury, also admitted that Christ had given a primacy to St. Peter.[11]

Prior to the post-Vatican II ecumenical dialogue, with its willingness to evaluate positively the papacy, Dom Gregory Dix, an Anglican monk, was an outspoken defender of the dominical institution of Petrine primacy. According to Dix, Mt 16 and the other Petrine texts testify to the dominical conferral of a true jurisdictional primacy upon Peter. The head of the apostles had exercised an important authority in the early community; furthermore, "it was the unchallenged belief everywhere in that period that the authority and function had been conveyed to him by our Lord himself."[12]

More recently, John Macquarrie has affirmed that the New Testament can substantiate giving to Peter a "certain primacy" among the other apostles.[13] Macquarrie's problem is not the dominical institution of a Petrine ministry but the meaning of the role given to Peter. Eric Mascall also holds that Petrine primacy was instituted by Christ,[14] but he is unhappy with the kind of jurisdictional primacy now claimed by the Popes and ratified by Vatican I: it is not the same as that known and exercised in the early Church. John de Satgé is another more recent advocate of a scripturally based Petrine primacy. He observes that "the fact that all the principal New Testament sources single out Peter among his colleagues, combined with the persistent sense of the later Church that there was something special about him, inclines many Christians today to take seriously a Petrine ministry."[15] But de Satgé does not speak for all his colleagues.

Other Anglican theologians reject a scriptural witness for any kind of Petrine primacy. Frederick Grant, for example, has stated that the real difficulty presented by Catholic teaching on the papacy is not the exercise of primatial authority, but the grounds on which it is justified. He opposes any scriptural argument from the Petrine texts to legitimate papal primacy. The problem, he says, is "the violence done to the New Testament in every attempt to defend the primacy as an institution dating from the first century and founded by Christ himself."[16] His opinion is echoed by others. Geoffrey Lampe is convinced that the Petrine texts should be jettisoned as a foundation for papal primacy since they "never had anything to do with the papacy in any case."[17] R. T. Beckwith is equally insistent that "neither the Lord's words to Peter, nor anything else in the New Testament can give it [papal primacy] warrant."[18] These theologians are unenthusiastic about the "Romanizing" scriptural interpretations espoused by some of their Anglican colleagues.

Thus, certain Anglicans are indeed willing to re-evaluate the papacy in relation to its Petrine foundation. They concede that at least a seed of the later papal ministry can be identified in the role that Jesus conferred on Peter. Others, however, though equally well-disposed to the papacy as an institution, do not accept any basis for its derivation from the will of the historical Jesus. It can, they say, only be legitimated on other grounds.

Anglican-Catholic Dialogue

In March 1982 the Anglican-Roman Catholic International Commission (ARCIC), whose members were bishops and theologians appointed by both communions, published their Final Report which they had already sent to their respective ecclesiastical authorities. The Report contains the commission's joint statements on eucharistic doctrine, ministry and ordination, and authority in the Church, as well as elucidations on the documents. The question of papal primacy is dealt with in *Authority in the Church I* (the Venice Statement of 1976), in the *Elucidation* of 1981 commenting on this statement, and in *Authority in the Church II* (the Windsor Statement of 1981). The publication of this Final Report marks the end of a first but important phase in the long search for reconciliation between the Anglican Communion and the Catholic Church.

ARCIC was an official body, but its reports are merely consultative and do not necessarily represent the authoritative teachings of either Anglicans or Catholics. The Final Report is a study document which both the archbishop of Canterbury and the Pope are to examine before any steps can be taken to act on the commission's conclusion which "calls for the establishing of a new relationship between our churches as a next stage in the journey toward Christian unity." Although widely hailed as an ecumenical event of great significance and possibly the major achievement of all bilateral dialogues since Vatican II, the Final Report does not solve even all the dogmatic questions raised in its treatment of its own agenda. Dr. Robert Runcie, the archbishop of Canterbury, has made it clear that the Report did not obligate Anglicans to accept Vatican I's definitions of papal jurisdiction and infallibility, while Cardinal Joseph Ratzinger, on behalf of the Vatican's Congregation for the Doctrine of the Faith, has written that "it is not yet possible to say that an agreement which is truly 'substantial' has been reached on the totality of questions studied by the Commission."

Three features of ARCIC's way of approaching Anglican-Catholic difficulties bear on the disputed question of papal primacy. First, the members were predisposed to go beyond the controversies of the sixteenth century to Scripture and the ancient Christian tradition. Thus, positions thought to be mutually contradictory have proved to be complementary. Second, ARCIC based its ecclesiology on the New Testament concept of *koinonia* or communion so that the Church is a universal communion of which the Eucharist is the efficacious sign, the episcopacy is the bond, and the universal primate is its visible link and focus. Third, and most significantly, ARCIC sought "to get behind the habit of thought and expression born and nourished in enmity and controversy," as Pope John Paul II remarked to the members of the Commission, in order to "pursue *together* that restatement of doctrine which new times and conditions are, as we both recognize, regularly calling for" (Preface to the Final Report). They did not intend to evade doctrinal difficulties but only controversial and polemical terminology.

Venice Statement (1976)

The traditional starting point of nearly every discussion between Anglicans and Catholics on papal primacy has been whether the Scriptures attest to its institution by Christ. In its joint statement, *Authority in the Church I* (1976), ARCIC does not deal at any length with the Petrine foundation for the papacy. It explicitly mentions the

Petrine texts only once and then simply to comment that their interpretation remains an outstanding question for future dialogue. In the
past, the members remark, "Catholics have put a greater weight on
the Petrine texts (Mt 16:18; Lk 22:31–32; Jn 21:15–17) than they are
generally thought to be able to bear" (#24a). Both the Anglican and
the Catholic participants criticize their own earlier polemical interpretations and conclude that it is no longer "necessary to stand by
former exegesis of these texts in every respect" (#24a). While the
commission draws attention to its shared opinion on the inadequacy
of a certain kind of apologetical exegesis, it suggests no acceptable
alternative interpretation.

Without citing any scriptural texts, the main body of the statement treats only once the Petrine foundation for papal claims. Here,
however, ARCIC's affirmation is deliberately ambiguous: "The importance of the bishop of Rome among his brother bishops, as explained by analogy with the position of Peter among the apostles,
was interpreted as Christ's will for his Church" (#12). The commission specifies neither when this analogy was first applied nor who has
accepted its validity. In spite of this allusion to Peter's role, the participants in fact provide no New Testament argument for the origin
of the papacy.

Two opposing reactions characterized critical reaction to *Authority in the Church I*. On the one hand, most Anglicans, as well as
a few Catholics, praised its omission of any biblical foundation for
the papacy. On the other hand, many Catholics were dissatisfied
with ARCIC's neglect of its Petrine justification. These criticisms
undoubtedly influenced the fuller treatment of this question in the
Windsor Statement.

According to most Anglican commentators, the commission deliberately jettisoned the Petrine texts as witnesses to a scriptural basis
for papal primacy because it recognized the weakness of this traditional justification for the papacy. Sharing this view, for example,
was Archbishop E. W. Scott, primate of the Anglican Church of
Canada, who thought that a significant contribution of the Venice
Statement was its acknowledgment that papal primacy "does not
simply flow automatically and inevitably from certain Petrine
texts."[19] A few Catholic critics shared their Anglican colleagues'
views that in the past the Petrine texts were given greater promi-

nence than they deserve. Peter Hebblethwaite, for example, cited approvingly the American Lutheran-Catholic Dialogue's criticism of apologetical exegesis as anachronistic because it reads too much into the scriptural texts. Consequently, he considered the omission of a Petrine foundation for papal primacy to be neither serious nor an obstacle to authentic dialogue.[20] In light of the Windsor Statement, however, such approval of ARCIC's original silence on the Petrine foundation of the papacy turned out to be premature.

For their part most Catholic commentators were unhappy with the commission's non-committal position on the Petrine basis for a universal ministry. Ceasing to justify the papacy with a scriptural argument, they thought, would obscure its dogmatic importance. Cuthbert Rand, for instance, noted the ambiguity which followed from ARCIC's presentation. Did the members agree or not in #12 that the analogy of Peter's role in the apostolic college correctly explains the relation of the Pope to the other bishops? It would have been preferable, and more in keeping with traditional Catholic theology, he said, to begin with the New Testament evidence for Petrine primacy. On the basis of recent exegesis, which increasingly supports a dominically instituted Petrine ministry, Rand criticized ARCIC's omission.[21] According to most Catholic theologians, ecumenical dialogue simply cannot afford to gloss over the relationship between Jesus and Peter in discussing the dogmatic basis for papal primacy. Their advice was subsequently heeded by ARCIC, as the Windsor Statement testifies.

Windsor Statement (1981)

In its attempt to clear up serious obstacles concerning the origin and succession of a Petrine ministry, *Authority in the Church II* pays a great deal of attention to the Petrine texts (#2–9). Taking into account the many suggestions made by critics of the Venice Statement, the commission studied what Catholics hold to be the scriptural foundation for papal primacy in order to shed light on the analogy that is drawn between the role of Peter among the apostles and that of the Pope among his fellow bishops (#2, 5). Any serious treatment of the papacy must decide whether or not such an analogy is justified from the New Testament evidence.

Without using the terminology, ARCIC leaves no doubt that a Petrine "primacy" is biblically warranted. "The New Testament," it says, "attributes to Peter a special position among the Twelve" (#3). The commission then summarizes the major scriptural texts referring to Peter, which when taken together "provide a general picture of his prominence" during the public ministry of Jesus and then later in the life of the early community (#3). Despite his being rebuked by Jesus and his betrayal of the Lord, "in the eyes of the New Testament writers," ARCIC concludes, "Peter holds a position of special importance" (#5).

The commission admits that these texts may not contain Jesus' authentic words to Peter, but it still maintains that it was Christ's will "to root the Church in the apostolic witness and mandate," within which Peter held his special role (#3). Nor did Peter assume this function on his own authority. Rather, as the statement notes, "this was not due to his own gifts and character," but it was "because of his particular calling by Christ" (#5). Quite clearly the Windsor Statement vindicates those who hold for a dominically willed Petrine role testified to in the New Testament.

At the same time, however, ARCIC is careful to point out that the Scriptures provide a basis not only for primacy but also for collegial cooperation or conciliarity. After summarizing the texts dealing with Peter's special role, it immediately adds that "responsibility for pastoral leadership was not restricted to Peter" (#4). Neither "binding and loosing" (Mt 16:19) nor serving as a "foundation" (Mt 16:18) is Peter's prerogative alone but is shared with all the apostles (Mt 18:18; Eph 2:20). Certainly the "distinctive features of Peter's ministry are stressed" in the New Testament, but "this ministry is that of an apostle and does not isolate him from the ministry of the other apostles" (#5). Primacy is tempered by collegiality; Peter remains in the apostolic group.

On March 29, 1982 the Vatican's Congregation for the Doctrine of the Faith published its observations on the Final Report of ARCIC. With respect to the commission's interpretation of Scripture, the congregation notes that the role of Peter described "does not measure up to the truth of faith as this has been understood by the Catholic Church on the basis of the principal Petrine texts of the New Testament." Nor does it "satisfy the requirements of the dogmatic statement of Vatican Council I" (#3:1). The congregation cites *Pastor Aeternus* to remind Catholics of the nature of Peter's "special position" as a "true and proper primacy of jurisdiction" (DS 3055). According to the official Roman response, the meaning of the dominically instituted Petrine primacy is not specified clearly enough in the Windsor Statement for it to be considered a full presentation of Catholic teaching on the Petrine texts.

Although not all Anglicans will accept a scriptural, and even a dominical, foundation for Peter's prominence in the life of the early Church, the very fact that an ecumenical commission of theologians and churchmen has reached this conclusion is remarkable. If officially accepted, it will in effect wipe away the major difficulty between Anglicans and Catholics concerning the Petrine foundation of a universal primacy. Such acceptance would not necessarily mean, of course, similar agreement on whether the bishop of Rome succeeds to the Petrine role. To that question we now turn.

Notes

1. "The Catholic Understanding of Office in the Church," *Theological Studies* 30 (1969) 568.

2. *Why We Need the Pope* (St. Meinrad, 1975) 93–100.

3. *La primauté pontificale: La doctrine de Vatican I—les voies d'une révision* (Gembloux, 1972) 167.

4. Joseph A. Burgess, *A History of the Exegesis of Matthew 16:17–19 from 1781 to 1965* (Ann Arbor, 1976) 160–161.

5. *Idem,* "Lutherans and the Papacy: A Review of Some Basic Issues," in *A Pope for All Christians?* ed. Peter J. McCord (New York, 1976) 24–27.

6. *Evangelischer Erwachsenenkatechismus,* ed. Werner Jentsch *et al.* (Gütersloh, 1975) 916.

7. "Einheit der Kirche als Glaubenswirklichkeit und als ökumenisches Ziel," *Unam Sanctam* 30 (1975) 220.

8. Paul C. Empie and T. Austin Murphy, eds., *Papal Primacy and the Universal Church: Lutherans and Catholics in Dialogue 5* (Minneapolis, 1974) 9–42. The following references in the text give the section number common to all translations. Unfortunately, the

numbering in the above edition is faulty: part 2 begins with #28 and not #35 as it should. I have used the corrected version which corresponds to other editions.

9. Armitage Robinson, "The Position of St. Peter in the Primitive Church: A Summary of the New Testament Evidence," in *The Conversations at Malines 1921–1925,* ed. Lord Halifax (London, 1930) 101.

10. *The Roman Primacy to A.D. 461* (London, 1936) 154.

11. *The Gospel and the Catholic Church* (London, 1936) 64.

12. *Jurisdiction in the Early Church* (1938; rpt. London, 1975) 101; cf 99–102.

13. *Principles of Christian Theology,* 2nd ed. (New York, 1977) 413.

14. *The Recovery of Unity* (London, 1958) 197–213.

15. *Peter and the Single Church* (London, 1980) 4.

16. *Rome and Reunion* (New York, 1965) 7.

17. "Authority in the Church: A Speech in Synod in February 1977," *Theology* 80 (1977) 363.

18. "Papal Authority in a Reunited Church?" *Faith & Unity* 20 (1976) 49.

19. "Reassess Authority of Pope and Primate," *Globe and Mail* (Toronto) February 14, 1977, 7.

20. "Anglican-Roman Catholic Agreement?" *Commonweal* 104 (1977) 108.

21. "The Agreed Statement on Authority: A Catholic Comment," *One in Christ* 13 (1977) 187–189.

3
Peter and the Pope

A growing awareness regarding the New Testament foundation for Petrine primacy marks only the first step in ecumenical discussion on the papacy. Even if theologians agree that Jesus gave to Peter a special ministry, another question must still be answered: Did anyone inherit this ministry from Peter, and, if so, on what grounds is such a succession demonstrated? We are now asking whether the papacy, as the present-day realization of Petrine primacy, is divinely willed, even if it is not of dominical institution. How then is the Pope related to Peter?

Catholics

Traditional Catholic doctrine deduces the permanence of the papacy from Christ's will for the permanence of the Church. Succession in the primacy of Peter is, accordingly, neither an accident of history nor simply a need of the community but the revealed will of Christ. A number of recent historical studies, however, have resulted in new interpretations of Vatican I's teaching on Petrine succession. On the one hand, a few Catholic theologians, the functionalists whose views we saw in the last chapter, now deny that the papacy, as a ministry succeeding to the role of Peter, is in any special way divinely willed. On the other hand, besides those theologians who simply repeat the conventional dogmatic formulations, many others have integrated this recent historical research into a theology of the papacy so that they still hold it to be divinely willed. Nonetheless, this second group clearly differentiates *divine* institution from *dominical* institution, a terminological refinement not consistently observed by earlier Catholic theologians.

Papacy Without Peter: A Functional Reality

Küng and Ohlig are among those theologians who, having determined that if historical and exegetical studies can prove that an ecclesial structure was not established immediately and directly by the historical Jesus, therefore hold such an institution to be only of human origin. It is divinely willed only in the widest sense of the word. In light of modern research the functionalists are able, consequently, to question the divine institution of many structures, not least of which is the papacy.

They do not, however, regard the papacy as a degeneration from the original message of Christ. For Küng, Hasenhüttl and Ohlig, developments in the Church's hierarchical constitution were legitimate and even necessary. Although the papacy cannot be justified by an appeal to Jesus' will, it need not, for that reason, be considered an ecclesial aberration.

Küng, for instance, admits the legitimacy of the papacy. It is a ministry which is *praeter evangelium,* that is, a development "beyond the Gospel" which can be tolerated but not absolutized. He has no reason to oppose on principle an office of unity for the Church and admits, in *On Being a Christian,* that the papacy is "not *a priori* contrary to Scripture. Whatever the value of arguments which may be adduced in its favor, there is nothing in Scripture to exclude such a ministerial primacy."[1] Whereas non-Catholic theologians have traditionally concluded from their interpretation of the Scriptures that the papacy is *contra evangelium,* or "contrary to the Gospel," the functionalists find no conclusive biblical argument either for it or against it.

When a theologian rejects the dominical foundation of the papacy, yet still gives it a place in the Church's structure, he must justify its role on other grounds. The early structures of the Church, including the papacy, did not originate with the will of the historical Jesus but came about because the community needed some organizational structures in order to survive. According to the functionalists, therefore, Petrine succession in the papacy emerged solely for historical, political, sociological and cultural reasons.

The development of papal primacy can best be explained, according to Ohlig in *Why the Church Needs the Pope,* as a response to the third-century Church's need for a center of unity: "On the basis of any other criterion than that of pastoral-theological efficiency, it does not seem possible to justify the primacy of the Roman bishop as an element in the structure of a particular Church."[2] Furthermore, the church at Rome had no single bishop as head of its community until the mid-second century. Because direction of the Roman church was in the hands of a collegial body, no position was open for a bishop to succeed personally to Peter during that time.[3]

Moreover, historical research has failed to provide any evidence before the third century that the bishop of Rome interpreted the Petrine texts in reference to himself as successor of Peter. This is further reason for the functionalists' believing the Petrine character of the Roman See to be a later invention. When the bishop of Rome first invoked these texts, they provided "a theological justification of a factual situation which had come about earlier and for other reasons."[4] Thus, these functionalists believe historical research proves that for a century there was no bishop at Rome who could personally succeed to Peter, and that later, when there was a monarchical bishop, he failed to claim, at least for a century, to be the successor of the apostle. In their opinion, Catholic tradition and theology are therefore mistaken in defending the idea of an uninterrupted succession to the primacy of Peter by the bishop of Rome.

In addition to doubting the historical fact of Petrine succession in the Roman See, the functionalists also deny that the Holy Spirit guided the emergence of the papacy in any special way. Except in the broadest sense, as could be claimed even for an institution such as the cardinalate, Petrine succession is not divinely willed. The papacy is, therefore, entirely a product of human history, forged by human decisions in a community continually in transformation. The papacy is only a human institution, they say, and has no claim to divine origin in any privileged sense.

Papacy with Peter: A Theological Reality

Unlike the functionalists, the majority of theologians emphasize that the only satisfactory Catholic justification for the papacy lies in showing that this is "an intrinsic element in the *mysterion* of God's eternal purpose for man in Jesus Christ."[5] As a theological reality the papal ministry must be viewed in light of the mystery of Christ and his Church.

Most Catholic theologians, nonetheless, recognize the role of human factors at the origin of the papacy as an historical and sociological institution. This large and influential group of theologians, which includes Yves Congar, Avery Dulles, Heinrich Fries, Walter Kasper, James McCue, Kilian McDonnell and Karl Rahner, recognize that the papacy emerged gradually in the first century of the Church's life. Kilian McDonnell summarizes their point of view: "The emergence and development of the Petrine office is seen as the result of the inter-action over an extended period of time of both theological and non-theological factors."[6] Certainly the institution which developed was "founded fundamentally by Jesus and guided by the Holy Spirit, but also subject to an extended historical process."[7] Nevertheless, as we shall discuss below, they still must answer the question: How does a Catholic theologian who accepts papal primacy account for the lapse of time between the institution of Petrine primacy by Christ and the explicit claim of the bishop of Rome that he was the successor of Peter, a consciousness not usually dated earlier than the mid-third century?

1. Gradual Emergence of the Papacy

Traditionally, theologians assumed that after the death of Peter every bishop of Rome was aware of the special authority which he inherited as the successor of the chief apostle. Although this succession of the bishop of Rome to the chair of Peter had not been universally recognized in the earliest centuries, it was sufficiently testified to in the writings of the Fathers. Catholic apologists explained the paucity of historical evidence for the exercise of Petrine authority on the grounds that there was little reason for its use. Nonetheless, primatial Petrine authority, they said, was "always 'there,' claimed and recognized, just waiting to come into greater prominence."[8] This traditional explanation emphasized the continuity between the promise and conferral of Petrine primacy by Christ and its perpetuity in the Pope. No Catholic apologist maintained that there was a time when papal primacy did not exist.

Contemporary theologians, however, are more sensitive than earlier apologists to the problems posed by the lack of conclusive documentation from the early Church. They are reluctant to build their dogmatic explanations on a questionable historical foundation. Like the textual critics, many theologians take the most difficult reading of the available data. They do not thereby necessarily deny the apologetic value of the testimony of the early Fathers such as Clement of Rome, Ignatius of Antioch and Irenaeus. So much the better if these Fathers can provide a witness for the exercise and recognition of papal primacy in the primitive Church! Nonetheless, the meaning of their writings is so disputed that these Fathers do not provide the desired historical proof for the continuity between Petrine and papal primacy.

Once scholars have accepted, as Church historian James McCue does, that "there seems to be no reason to suppose a priori that the post-apostolic Church was immediately in such full possession of itself, of its own structure, that it immediately asserted (or assented to) the doctrine of the primacy of the bishop of Rome,"[9] do they therefore conclude that the papacy is merely a human institution? The majority of theologians do not think so. Just as a certain amount of time was required for the formation of the scriptural canon, so a certain amount of time was required for shaping definitive ecclesial structures. The primatial function of the bishop of Rome emerged slowly. Yet, as Patrick Granfield summarizes this position, "since this development was directed by God and manifested a decisive and enduring element in the Church, it can be said to be divinely instituted."[10]

Since a decentralized episcopacy seemed to function adequately in the early post-apostolic community, no particular office of unity was then required. According to McCue and others, the need for the papacy arose when divisions in the episcopacy made it apparent that a single head of the body of bishops was necessary for the good of the Church.[11] At this time the bishop of Rome began to fulfill the ministry which Jesus had conferred on Peter. The need for a leader led to rereading the Scriptures in light of this historical experience: the churches recognized that the bishop of Rome had *de facto* fulfilled the Petrine office of "strengthening the brethren" (cf Lk 22:32) and that this task would permanently devolve upon him. Only at this point did appeal to Jesus' words to Peter become the foundation for justifying the papacy.

The Church did not invent the papacy as a means of securing its unity. Rather, it recognized in the commission of Christ that Jesus had provided an office for guaranteeing the unity of the Church and that the Pope fulfilled the same function in the episcopal college which Peter had carried out in the apostolic college. Consequently, the primatial office was not "present" in the early Church from the outset. The historical papacy emerged at a later date when it was needed to fulfill the purpose for which it had been established.

Most Catholic theologians now accept the complex interplay of divine and historical human factors at the origin of papal primacy. They commonly agree that a certain correlation, but not causal relationship, existed between Rome's status as the capital of the Empire and the emergence of the leading role of its bishop.[12] Just as Rome was the center of unity for the Empire, and the emperor its personification, so did the unity of the universal Church come to focus on the Roman community and its bishop. Still other factors complement this political one. The church at Rome, say these theologians, gained considerable prestige from its renown for charity and fidelity in persecution. Theologians therefore no longer minimize these influences but endeavor to interpret them in a way which respects both historical research and Catholic dogma.

2. Divine Institution: Guided by the Spirit

If the development of papal primacy is interpreted in light of the Holy Spirit's guidance of the Church, then the presence of human factors at its origin does not rule out the papacy's "divine" institution. Most Catholic theologians no longer restrict the meaning of the divine institution of papal primacy to its immediate establishment by the historical Jesus. They now believe that the creative activity of the Holy Spirit powerfully present in the early Church also manifests the divine will. Raymond Brown says that when the Church holds a structure to have been instituted by Christ, this affirmation "can be defended in the nuanced sense that . . . [it] gradually emerged in a Church that stemmed from Christ and that this emergence was (in the eyes of faith) guided by the Holy Spirit."[13] Merely because a structure was not immediately established by Jesus does not imply that it is, for that reason, only a human institution. The majority of Catholic theologians still contend that the papacy is of divine institution, that is, it is in conformity with Scripture and ultimately rooted in the word of God, even though its historical form came into being as a result of a free decision of the post-apostolic Church. These Catholic theologians draw attention to the unity of the will of Christ and of his Spirit. They invoke the divine will as the basis of an ecclesial structure, even when biblical criticism has proved that Jesus himself left no detailed blueprint for structuring the community.[14]

The reason for continuing to hold the divine, but not dominical, institution of the papacy is its pneumatological foundation. According to these scholars, the papacy's emergence followed historical and sociological processes. At the origin of this development, however, was the Petrine primacy conferred by Jesus. Furthermore, the subsequent evolution of the papal ministry was guided by the intervention of the Holy Spirit. The papacy therefore should be considered simultaneously as the fruit of the Spirit and as the result of a sociological-historical process.

But how do we know whether this historical emergence of the papacy really corresponds to God's will or not? The functionalists assert that this structural development occurred as a natural historical process, not as God's plan for the Church. The majority, however, emphasize that faith is needed to discern the divine will in history. Even when the historical arguments upon which an assertion is based are themselves not compelling, an institution can nonetheless be positively related to the divine will. Avery Dulles notes in this regard that "in faith we can affirm the positive relationship of certain historical structures of the Church to the will of God, but the grounds for that affirmation are not fully cogent outside of the commitment of faith itself."[15] Acceptance of papal primacy ultimately rests on a conviction of faith. Thus, for most Catholic theologians the papacy shares in the mystery of the Church and is an object of faith.

Lutherans

Reinterpreting the Reformation Polemic

The rejection of Petrine primacy by Luther and in the confessional writings is so unambiguous that it seems to present an insurmountable obstacle even to discussing a biblical foundation for the papacy. While an authentically Lutheran understanding must be based on these classical sources, not everyone accepts their authority to the same extent and in the same way.

The increasingly influential group of revisionist Lutheran theologians are reappraising their theological tradition. Although the confessional writings resound with a strongly anti-papal tone, they also leave open, as the revisionists remind us, the possibility for a reformed papacy. Within Lutheranism there is already an authentic, but largely forgotten, openness to papal primacy.

Lutherans base their re-evaluation of the papacy on three factors. First, they have developed a new ecclesiology which gives more importance to the visible structures of the Church. Second, Lutherans now read their confessional writings in their historical context. Third, many suggest that the reformers wanted to reject only the way in which the Pope exercised primatial authority and not the papal office itself.

Since the Reformation, Lutherans had denied the possibility of considering any specific ministerial institution of the visible Church to be dominically established. The change began in the 1930s when the rise of the un-Christian Nazi state revealed the impotence of a totally spiritual and non-juridical ecclesiology. Some theologians and churchmen came to recognize that empirical manifestations of the Church could belong to its essence. The visibility of an institution was no longer in itself sufficient reason for holding it to be only of human origin or of human right. Because of this new ecclesiological view theologians opened the way, at least indirectly, for a re-evaluation of the papacy, an institution very much part of the visible Church.

Secondly, revisionist Lutherans now generally agree that, like all historical documents, the works of Luther and the confessional writings must be interpreted in their original context. Sixteenth-century assertions describing the Pope as the antichrist, for example, no longer correspond to twentieth-century Lutheran convictions about the bishop of Rome.[16] In their polemical writings the reformers emphasized their hatred of the papacy and their struggle against the Popes. But contemporary writers attribute to the papacy neither such a central nor such a negative role in their theology: papal primacy is not a doctrine on which the Church stands or falls.

For these present-day thinkers, Luther's polemic against papal primacy belongs solely to the historically-conditioned dimension of the Reformation. Even though at that time his position was justified, Luther's anti-papal arguments do not touch, as Wolfhart Pannenberg says, the authentic core of his reform doctrine.[17] According to the revisionists, the Reformation controversy on the papacy was primarily concerned with the Pope's relationship to the word of God. For Lutherans, the Gospel alone enjoys primacy in the Church: all authority is subject to and limited by God's word. Because the Pope had placed himself over the word of the Gospel, the reformers were convinced that he had apostatized. They saw themselves in the awkward position of having a Pope who did not teach an orthodox doctrine of justification, a belief necessary for salvation, and who declared them heretical for holding it. To safeguard this fundamental doctrine, considered to be the very heart of the Gospel, the reformers had to reject the divine institution of the papacy and so free themselves from the obligation to accept the Pope's teaching.

The historical conditioning of the confessional writings is made clear by yet a third argument: the reformers opposed the way in which the Pope exercised his primatial authority but not the papacy itself. They attacked the personal corruption and immorality of certain Popes because such scandalous conduct hampered preaching the Gospel. At times their criticism was so harsh that it led them to question the legitimacy of the papacy itself.

Harding Meyer holds, for example, that when the reformers denied the Catholic understanding they did not intend to imply that the papacy was just a human invention or an "invention of the devil." They used strong and even offensive expressions only to correct an exaggerated and maximalist interpretation of papal authority: the intervention of the Pope in temporal affairs and the necessity of submission to the Pope as a requirement for salvation. Meyer is certain that Melanchthon did not wish to contest the divine right of the papacy, and hence the existence of an original Petrine primacy, but only wanted to insist on the need to exercise papal authority in a way different from that which Catholics accepted in the sixteenth century.[18] The revisionist theologians hold that the reformers criticized the historical papacy familiar to them because they hoped it would be reformed in light of the word of God. Consequently, previous polemics do not hinder reconsidering papal primacy as an authentic ecclesial ministry.

Papacy and Providence

Only those Lutheran theologians who accept some kind of Petrine primacy bother to address the question whether the Pope succeeds to the role Peter held in the apostolic Church. Among those revisionists who accept Petrine primacy, however, problems still arise touching on two related issues: the fact of succession and how this fact is to be interpreted—whether the papacy is only a socio-political institution or whether it is providentially guided.

Even Lutheran theologians who accept a biblically warranted Petrine primacy fail to acknowledge the bishop of Rome as the only personal successor to Peter. The Scriptures, they say, do not indicate that Peter's primacy was to continue personally in a successor. Some of the revisionists do admit that Christ gave Peter a unique ministry and that the bishop of Rome legitimately enjoyed a ministry of direction in the early Church. They do not, however, posit a divinely willed connection between Petrine primacy and papal primacy. When the Popes claimed that their ministry alone succeeded to that of Peter, such a development was illegitimate. In other words, the real difficulty for Lutherans begins when the Pope is considered the only bearer of the role Jesus assigned to Peter.

Not only did Luther and Melanchthon deny that the bishop of Rome succeeded to an original Petrine primacy but they also argued that papal primacy developed owing to purely human reasons. Many Lutheran theologians still accept this position, while the more ecumenically minded are willing to consider the possibility that, although human factors were responsible for the historical development of the papacy, their presence need not mean that it can only be justified in the same way as secular political structures. Recently several revisionist theologians, such as Joseph Burgess and George Lindbeck, have conceded that the emergence of the papacy was somehow providentially assisted. This concession opens the way for serious ecumenical dialogue on Petrine succession.

Burgess proposes that Lutherans, while remaining faithful to their tradition, can accept that the papacy exists "in accordance with God's will." Although this does not mean that Christ instituted the papacy by a juridical act, it does mean that God wills whatever is necessary for the Church to function as the preacher of God's word. In speaking of the papacy Burgess admits that "the structures that have developed in the Church are God's will, first of all because they are in the Bible, but also because God cares for his Church."[19] When a theologian invokes this special providential assistance, then the papacy need not be considered only a human institution.

It is, therefore, no longer unthinkable for Lutheran theologians to grant that the guidance of the Holy Spirit can be discerned in the development of the papacy and in the Pope's claim to be the successor of St. Peter. To insist that the papacy emerged as an historical institution does not necessarily negate their considering that it carries out a divine mission for the good of the Church. Like many Catholic theologians, these Lutheran writers recognize the validity of this pneumatological foundation for the papacy as sufficient for believing it to be of divine, though not dominical, institution.

Lutheran-Catholic Dialogue

The American Lutheran-Catholic Dialogue reflects the newer understanding of the origin of papal primacy and its relationship to Petrine primacy that theologians have developed in recent years. The Catholic participants concede that the emergence of the papacy depends not only on Christ's commission to Peter but also on historical and human factors (#51, 52), whereas the Lutherans concede that the Petrine texts played a definite role. Thus, both sides agree that the embodiment of Petrine primacy in a single person or office resulted from a long process of development which began in the apostolic Church (#21).

In their bilateral statement on the emergence of papal primacy, the Dialogue partners affirm that "the papal office can be seen both as a response to the guidance of the Spirit in the Christian community, and also as an institution which, in its human dimensions, is tarnished by frailty and even unfaithfulness" (#21). Both Lutherans and Catholics agree that the evolution of the papacy must be evaluated by taking into account the assisting intervention of the Holy Spirit.

In line with recent revisionist thought, the Lutheran members of the Dialogue do not hold the historical papacy to be of divine institution (#28, 40, 45). As for the Catholic participants, they reflect the consensus of the Catholic theological community at large and not that of the functionalists. Although the papacy as an institution may well have emerged later than was previously thought to be the case, they still consider it to be the "divinely willed sequel" to the function exercised by Peter in the apostolic college (#53). The papacy, they repeat, is, "in a true sense, 'divinely instituted' " (#49) and "an institution in accordance with God's will" (#30).

Most Catholic critics of *Differing Attitudes Toward Papal Primacy* find nothing objectionable in the bilateral statement's view that historical factors conditioned the emergence of papal primacy. Reactions of noted theologians confirm that the alternative of holding the papacy to be either of divine institution or of human institution is a choice unable to do justice to the complex origins of papal primacy.

Charles Moeller, secretary of the Vatican's Secretariat for Promoting Christian Unity, thinks, for example, that the question of the papacy's origin "goes *beyond* a mere alternative between a purely human and a purely divine foundation."[20] Because of the position agreed upon in the common statement, the Lutheran belief in a papacy of human institution is therefore no longer so radically opposed to the Catholic belief in a papacy of divine institution.

According to Yves Congar, the Lutherans' use of sixteenth-century reform texts describing the papacy as a human institution is a valid starting point in ecumenical dialogue. By the very fact of conceding that the papacy was a legitimate human institution and not from the devil, the Lutheran participants thereby admit that at some point in history the papacy served the good of the Church and therefore deserves to be considered, if only temporarily, a providential development. Congar asks whether the possibility of carrying out this positive role might not reappear in the Church. He suggests that the Lutheran theological tradition which qualifies such a papacy as a human institution readily admits a meaning compatible with Catholic belief. A papacy justified as an institution of human right can be thought of as "a providential human right, willed by God, and therefore in some way divine."[21]

Lutherans and Catholics, even of the mainline theological tradition, are moving closer together in their understanding of the origin of the papacy. Wide disagreement remains, as we shall see in the next chapter, on the consequences which each tradition draws from its view of the papacy as a providential development.

Anglicans

Pope Without a Petrine Connection

The classic and least ambiguous teaching on Petrine succession, which is held by most Anglicans, rejects outright that the Pope is the successor of Peter. Even theologians who accept Petrine primacy deny any perpetuity in the primacy Jesus granted to Peter. Peter, they maintain, was never bishop of Rome and had no successors in that See. Consequently, no bishop could succeed to his apostolic prerogatives.

The majority of Anglican theologians explain the *de facto* prominence of the Roman See as the result of a combination of human factors. Included among the reasons usually mentioned are the secular importance of Rome as the capital of the Empire, its dual apostolic foundation, its preservation of the relics of the martyred apostles Peter and Paul, its faithful preservation of Christ's teaching, the astuteness of its bishops, and the wealth, number, generosity and heroism of its members. These human factors alone explain the origin of papal primacy. They have no theological significance but serve rather to prove that the papacy is only a human institution.

Most contemporary Anglican theologians emphasize that the papacy is an institution justified on the grounds of expediency; they make a case for it on historical or pragmatic grounds. In his summary of attitudes toward papal primacy, J. Robert Wright explains that

Anglicans would be willing, "on the basis of historical contingencies but not by divine right, to recognize the See of Rome as the first (prime) See of Christendom."[22] Such a recognition of the papacy does not derive from a conviction that the Pope succeeds to Peter's primacy but from a simple acknowledgment that the church at Rome and its bishops came to enjoy an authoritative position in the universal Church in the same way that Canterbury was accorded a place of honor within the Anglican Communion.

Pope with a Petrine Connection

Some contemporary Anglican theologians, however, do accept that the Pope's ministry to the universal Church is related to that of Peter. A few even believe that the Pope is the successor of Peter. But most do not go that far, preferring instead a vaguer description of the Pope's relationship to the apostle.

As early as 1936 Michael Ramsey raised the question whether the Pope succeeds to Peter's role in the apostolic college: Is the papacy a legitimate development which grew out of a primacy which Christ had conferred on Peter?[23] Even though he himself did not reply to this question, Ramsey nonetheless opened the door to serious Anglican consideration of Petrine succession.

John Macquarrie has recently argued on historical and theological grounds that Peter went to Rome, served as bishop of the local church there, and enjoyed special privileges which he passed on to his successors in that See. Not all the questions about succession, he adds, can be answered with confidence. Some light is shed on the problem by considering the historical emergence of other ecclesial structures whose legitimacy is unquestioned. The development of the New Testament canon, of the sacraments, and of the structured ministry, for example, have origins as obscure as that of Roman primacy. Nonetheless, according to Macquarrie, the Church has accepted these developments as fully legitimate and necessary. It is, therefore, impossible simply to rule out the idea of Petrine succession on the grounds that it has no scriptural foundation.[24] To hold that the Pope is the successor of Peter is, he says, entirely compatible with Anglican ecclesiology.

As in the question of Petrine primacy, one of the most outspoken defenders of Petrine succession is Eric Mascall. He maintains that because the post-apostolic and the apostolic Church must be essentially the same, then Petrine succession should be allowed as a possibility.[25] In his recent book, *Peter and the Single Church,* John de Satgé expresses this same conviction that the apostolic function entrusted to Peter was meant to endure. The location of the Petrine ministry at Rome is secondary. He adds that "the Pope is what he is, not because he is the bishop of Rome, but because he fulfills the function of Peter who left Jerusalem, spent a period in Antioch, and arrived in Rome where he was martyred."[26] Very few Anglicans, however, go as far as Mascall and Satgé's explicit acceptance of personal Petrine succession.

More common are the theologians who relate the papacy to Peter without admitting that the Pope is the personal successor to the chief apostle. These Anglicans justify papal primacy on "religious," rather than on purely secular, grounds. They stress Rome as the site of the martyrdom of Sts. Peter and Paul; furthermore, since the second century, Rome's seniority and prestige have derived from its historical association with the two apostles.[27] Thus, the Pope's role in the Church is related historically and spiritually to Peter's, but it would be going too far to maintain that the bishop of Rome is the successor to Peter.

Many Anglicans who accept the Petrine connection as a basis for papal claims are, however, also willing to assign more than a sociological justification to the emergence of the papacy. An early and influential champion of the papacy as a divinely willed institution was Gregory Dix (†1952). He attacked the conventional Anglican argument that the papacy developed solely because of the secular importance of Rome. According to Dix, even though the practical consequences of papal authority were frequently debated in the early centuries, it never occurred to any Christian writer, Roman or non-Roman, either in defense or in attack, to legitimate the privileges of the Roman See on the basis of the secular position of Rome. The appearance of that idea at the Council of Constantinople (381) was an innovation. Furthermore, given the Christians' negative attitude to Rome, it was not at all "natural" that the capital city should be accorded a special role in the universal Church.[28] Few of Dix's Anglican colleagues would follow his presentation entirely, but he defended his theory as compatible with Anglican views on the papacy, and he paved the way for a more open attitude to papal primacy as a divinely guided institution.

Following Dix, some contemporary Anglicans also mention the divine assistance at the origin of the papacy. Like many Catholics and a few Lutherans, they draw attention to its pneumatological foundation. According to Arthur M. Allchin, there is a movement within Anglicanism which holds that "Rome is at least by divine permission, if not by divine right, indicated as the center of unity within the Christian family."[29] Such theologians, though a minority, come very close to a contemporary Catholic understanding of papal primacy as a divinely willed institution.

Anglican-Catholic Dialogue

Venice Statement (1976): Papacy and History

Despite its being a joint declaration, *Authority in the Church I* adopts a fundamentally Anglican interpretation of the origin of the papacy. The Anglican participants admit to more than their sixteenth-century predecessors did but to less than would some of their more pro-papal contemporaries. At the same time, the statement itself is ambiguous enough to satisfy the Catholic members of the commission, though most of their colleagues readily drew attention to its theological shortcomings in this regard.

In the early centuries, as ARCIC notes, the individual local churches, each presided over by a bishop, were gathered into regional and supra-regional groupings. As a result, a particular function of oversight *(episcope)* gradually devolved upon the bishops of the more prominent sees (#10). After describing the emergence of these regional, metropolitan and patriarchal primacies, the Venice Statement then outlines the origin of a universal primacy: "It is within the context of this historical development that the See of Rome, whose prominence was associated with the death there of Peter and Paul, eventually became the principal center in matters concerning the Church universal" (#12). The document leaves open the question whether the papacy should be justified theologically in the same way as regional primacies. Moreover, *Authority in the Church I* contains no explicit references either to the role of the Holy Spirit guiding this emergence of the historical papacy or to the bishop of Rome as the successor to St. Peter.

Anglican critics had no difficulty in accepting the papacy as a venerable historical institution, a view to which they saw themselves committed by the Venice Statement. Former archbishop of Canterbury Donald Coggan equated the papal primacy agreed to by ARCIC with a patriarchal primacy of universal scope. "The patriarchal role for the bishop of Rome, the Pope . . . does not worry me particularly," he said, "because on historic grounds, of course, there has been a bishop of Rome from the very, very early days, and it is very likely, if not certain, that Peter and Paul were both martyred there."[30] For Anglican commentators, therefore, the Venice Statement's description of the development of papal primacy confirmed their traditional understanding of its historical and human foundation.

George Tavard, a member of ARCIC, suggested that the Venice Statement raises a momentous question for fellow Catholics: "Can a Roman primacy which simply emerges from historical developments, but is not, even implicitly, taught in the Scriptures, do justice to the role of the Popes in the transmission of faith and to the doctrines of the two Vatican Councils?"[31] Unlike the Anglican critics of *Authority in the Church I,* Catholic commentators answered Tavard's question negatively. They found ARCIC's presentation of the historical foundation of the papacy and the interpretation given to it by most Anglicans to be an inadequate expression of Catholic teaching.

The Catholic critics discovered a major difficulty in the Venice Statement's implied comparison between the emergence of the regional primacies and of a universal primacy. This approach leaves the impression that the origin of the papacy is similar to that of regional primacies, the "result of a simple delegation of powers by local churches," said Christophe Dumont, "a delegation which does not of itself demand a particular mandate from on high."[32] The mere fact of the historical emergence of Roman primacy and its recognition by other churches, the commentators continued, cannot by itself securely establish Catholic doctrine. In a theology of the papacy, facts call for interpretation. The theologian must ask why such a development occurred: Is it an ideological superstructure to justify the acquisition of power and privilege, or a legitimate ecclesial develop-ment, or an evolution mandated by the very will of Christ? If the pa-pacy is justified only as a product of historical development, a position which *Authority in the Church I* implies, then papal primacy cannot be given its traditional dogmatic value. History is unable to determine what is revealed as God's will for his Church. According-ly, the great majority of Catholic commentators insisted that an authentic justification for the papacy would have to include recog-nizing the Pope as the successor of Peter and affirming the papacy's historical emergence as God's explicit will for the Church.

Windsor Statement (1981): Papacy and Providence

In *Authority in the Church II* (1981), ARCIC takes to heart es-pecially the Catholic criticisms of the Venice Statement. After agree-ing that Christ commissioned Peter to lead the apostles, the participants go on to discuss whether Peter's role was to continue in the post-apostolic Church. Three distinct questions can be separated in their treatment: first, they question whether a Petrine function can be transmitted; second, they ask who the successor is; third, they evaluate theologically this succession to Peter's ministry. No other bilateral ecumenical document has ever come so close to Catholic teaching on Petrine succession as defined in Chapter 2 of *Pastor Ae-ternus* (1870).

Was the ministry Peter fulfilled in the apostolic Church trans-ferable to later generations or was it absolutely unique? ARCIC con-cludes that "the New Testament contains no explicit record of a transmission of Peter's leadership" to the post-apostolic Church (#6). Given the scriptural lack of specificity regarding the transmis-sion of apostolic authority in general, this omission is not surprising. Nor has Catholic teaching ever held that Jesus himself either named or explicitly willed a successor to Peter.

Nonetheless, both Anglicans and Catholics accept the reality of apostolic succession—that bishops succeed to the office of the apos-tles. Consequently, ARCIC states that "what is true of the transmis-sibility of the mission of the apostolic group is true of Peter as a member of it" (#8). Just as the ministry of the apostles in and to the

Church continues in the college of bishops, so the ministry of Peter lasts as head of that college. It is true, of course, that the apostolic mission cannot be passed on in its entirety: the apostles are foundations and thus are "the unique, commissioned witnesses to the once-for-all saving work of Christ" (#8). In the same way, therefore, "Peter's role cannot be transmitted in its totality" to any successor (#8), but a ministry does survive in every generation which, to a certain degree, corresponds to the office of Peter in the New Testament. Already in the ancient Church this transmission of a Petrine ministry was justified on scriptural grounds because "the Fathers and Doctors of the Church gradually came to interpret the New Testament data as pointing in the same direction" (#7).

The Windsor Statement also identifies who did in fact succeed to Peter's ministry. From a consideration of the historical data, it concludes that Rome "came to be recognized as possessing a unique responsibility among the churches" and that the bishop of Rome "was seen to perform a special service in relation to the unity of the churches, and in relation to fidelity to the apostolic inheritance, thus exercising among his fellow bishops functions analogous to those ascribed to Peter, whose successor the bishop of Rome claimed to be" (#6). Certainly there is no divine mandate that the universal primacy be located in the Roman See, but "the original witness of Peter and Paul and the continuing exercise of a universal *episcope* by the See of Rome present a unique presumption in its favor" (*Elucidation,* #8). In fact, ARCIC accepts the historical linking of succession to the ministry of Peter with succession to the episcopacy of the Roman See, without however claiming that this relationship is itself divinely willed.

According to ARCIC, the emergence of the historical papacy is not a purely human development but one which "cannot be dissociated from the providential action of the Holy Spirit" (*Elucidation,* #8). Whereas the Venice Statement is unclear about qualifying theologically the development of the papacy, the Windsor Statement affirms that "it is possible to think that a primacy of the bishop of Rome is not contrary to the New Testament and is part of God's purpose regarding the Church's unity and catholicity" (#7). In light of the Catholic criticisms, the implied comparison between the development of Roman primacy and that of regional primacies was dropped in favor of a strong statement that the papacy is a gift of divine providence to the Church and not just an historical institution.

Authority in the Church II has made a significant contribution to ecumenical dialogue on the Petrine foundation of the papal ministry. We can conclude that insofar as evaluation of the past is concerned, no dogmatic differences separate the Catholic and Anglican positions on the emergence of the historical papacy. But what about the future? To recognize the providential guidance of Roman primacy in history is not necessarily to claim that it will forever remain a ministry in the Church. So now we must ask: Can there be a future Church without a Pope?

Notes

1. (Garden City, 1976) 496.

2. 112–113.

3. Ohlig, *Why We Need the Pope,* 37.

4. *Ibid.,* 92.

5. Cornelius Ernst, "The Primacy of Peter: Theology and Ideology," *New Blackfriars* 50 (1969) 349.

6. "Papal Primacy: Development, Centralization and Changing Styles," in *Papal Primacy and the Universal Church,* 175.

7. Norbert Brox, "Historical Problems concerning Papal Primacy," *Theological Digest* 26 (1978) 10–11.

8. James F. McCue, "The Roman Primacy in the Second Century and the Problem of the Development of Dogma," *Theological Studies* 25 (1964) 161.

9. *Ibid.,* 163.

10. *The Papacy in Transition* (Garden City, 1980) 102.

11. McCue, "Roman Primacy," 191.

12. Avery Dulles, "Papal Authority in Roman Catholicism," in *A Pope for All Christians?* ed. Peter J. McCord (New York, 1976) 53.

13. *Priest and Bishop: Biblical Reflections* (New York, 1970) 73.

14. Brown, *Biblical Reflections on Crises Facing the Church* (New York, 1975) 57–58.

15. "*Ius Divinum* as an Ecumenical Problem," *Theological Studies* 38 (1977) 695.

16. Wenzel Lohff, "Would the Pope Still Have Been the Antichrist for Luther Today?" in *Papal Ministry in the Church,* ed. Hans Küng, *Concilium* 64 (New York, 1971) 68–74.

17. "Reformation und Einheit der Kirche," *Unam Sanctam* 30 (1975) 178.

18. "L'ufficio papale nella visuale luterana," in *Papato e servizio petrino,* ed. Heinrich Stirnimann and Lukas Vischer (Alba, 1976) 77–79.

19. "Lutherans and the Papacy," 32.

20. "General Report," *Information Service: Secretariat for Promoting Christian Unity* 33 (1977) 3, 19.

21. "Bulletin de théologie," *Revue des Sciences Philosophiques et Théologiques* 59 (1975) 500.

22. "Anglicans and the Papacy," in *A Pope for All Christians?* 199.

23. *Gospel and the Church,* 64.

24. *Principles of Christian Theology,* 413.

25. *Recovery of Unity,* 197–201.

26. *Peter and the Single Church,* 37.

27. Lampe, "Authority in the Church," 347.

28. *Jurisdiction,* 110–116.

29. "Lambeth and the Papacy," *One in Christ* 5 (1969) 23.

30. "Reactions to the Venice Statement," *Ecumenical Trends* 6 (1977) 105.

31. "The Anglican-Roman Catholic Agreed Statements and Their Reception," *Theological Studies* 41 (1980) 92.

32. "Agreed Statement: A Critique and Analysis," *Origins* 6 (27 January 1977) 513.

4
Church Without a Pope?

The re-evaluation of Petrine primacy and Petrine succession inevitably leads to the further question: Do Catholics, Lutherans and Anglicans hold that the papacy fulfills so necessary a role in the Church that its acceptance is a *sine qua non* if full communion is to be restored between the churches? When all is said and done, do we really need the Pope? Contemporary theologians of the three traditions express a surprising amount of convergence, though not yet consensus, on the value and even the need for the papacy as a ministry at the service of the universal Church.

Catholics

Two main approaches to the question of the necessity of the papacy can be identified. On the one hand, the functionalist theologians, whom in this chapter we shall call "reversibilists," maintain that papal primacy is not permanently necessary to the Church. On the other hand, the majority of Catholic theologians, the "irreversibilists," including Yves Congar, Avery Dulles, Walter Kasper, Karl Rahner, and Leo Scheffczyk, hold that the papacy belongs to the very nature of the Church which Christ willed.

Reversibilists

Hasenhüttl, Ohlig and Küng accept the idea of the reversibility of a divinely willed institution. In principle, they say, the papacy is reversible. In practice, however, the Pope plays and undoubtedly will continue to play an important role in the life of the Church.

Reversibilist theologians argue that if an institution could have developed differently in the past, then it might be reversed in the future. The papacy, they say, came about as a result of free human decisions made by the early Church. Although it emerged as an effective way to hold the universal Church together, such a beginning in contingent historical choices is also the basis of its possible abolition in the future. Because this way of securing the unity of the Church results from one choice among various legitimate ones, such as a more collegial model, reversibilists conclude that the Church of subsequent generations is not permanently bound to a papal polity.

Hasenhüttl, for example, describes the Church's hierarchical structure as an auxiliary institution subordinate to the charismatic. He concludes that on the very grounds of being auxiliary, the papal-episcopal constitution is therefore reversible. Furthermore, because the papacy originated as a human response to a need for organization and unity among the churches, it does not belong to the Church's essence. The Church, therefore, neither stands nor falls with the papacy.[1]

Another argument for reversibility is based on the conviction that the Holy Spirit constantly provides the Church with the structures it needs. Although this pneumatological argument guarantees a divinely willed origin for the papacy, it also makes likely a change in the Church's future structure. The reversibilists therefore entertain the possibility that the papacy was willed as only a temporary institution. Though it was entirely legitimate at one time, it is not necessarily valid for all future ages. Reversibilists call into question the conventional assumption that whatever God has instituted, he intends to last forever. They suggest instead that perhaps Christ willed papal primacy for only a limited time. If it should happen at some point that the Pope no longer fulfills the function for which the office was designed, the papacy could then be justifiably abolished.[2]

Since, according to Hasenhüttl, there was a time in the early Church, and on occasion in other periods as well, when there was no Pope, such a situation could arise again in the future. Based on this historical precedent, the absence of the papal office does not therefore imply that the Church lacks a constitutive element. What traditional theology interprets as an anomalous and necessarily temporary situation—for the Church to be without a Pope—Hasenhüttl proposes as a model for future ecclesial polity. Quite simply, in Hasenhüttl's mind, the Church can do without the papal office.

Ohlig's views are similar to Hasenhüttl's. He, too, thinks that the papacy developed from historical contingencies. Like all ecclesial structures, the papacy can be transformed, though as an institution of venerable age and historical importance it cannot be arbitrarily abolished.[3] Nonetheless, papal primacy is not a permanent institution. The papacy remains legitimate only as long as it fulfills its function of serving the unity of the universal Church.

A somewhat more moderate, though still fundamentally reversibilist view, can be recognized in the writings of Hans Küng. According to him, developments in the Church which do not go back to the explicit will of Jesus revealed in the Scriptures are to be respected and not changed at will, but such institutions have no claim to permanence. Among these possibly reversible structures Küng includes the papacy.[4] Although he does state that "the Church, and perhaps Christianity as a whole, would lack something if this Petrine ministry were no longer there: something that is not inessential for the Church,"[5] Küng omits papal primacy from his list of permanent institutions constitutive of the Church. Without in any way actively promoting the idea, Küng, like Hasenhüttl, Ohlig and other reversibilists, would allow for an ecclesial polity without a Pope.

Irreversibilists

Notwithstanding the arguments of the reversibilists, most Catholic theologians still hold the papacy to be constitutive of the full reality of the Church. Recent scriptural and historical research has corrected, as we saw in Chapter 3, earlier understandings of the immediacy of the papacy's dominical institution, but it has not altered the Catholic consensus that papal primacy is absolutely necessary to the Church. Dulles sums up this contemporary view: "It may plausibly be argued that the papal office, as an embodiment of the Petrine ministry, even though it cannot be historically traced to the first generations, has won for itself an enduring place in the Church."[6] The papacy is permanent; that is, in the future it will never be replaced by another office which will succeed to the primacy of Peter.

These theologians have not dealt at length, however, with the reasons why the papacy is permanently necessary. Irreversibilists assert their conviction rather than demonstrate it. They believe that this irreversibility involves a question of truth about the nature of the Church, and they ground their belief in the classical argument: papal primacy is irreversible because the Church is permanent; thus, as long as the Church will last, so will the papacy. In his summary of this view Patrick Granfield says: "The papacy is an essential and permanent element of the Church of Christ, because it is willed by Christ. It has both a human and a divine foundation, but it is the latter that guarantees its permanence."[7]

When the irreversibilists affirm the necessity of the papacy they do so with a keen awareness of the difficulties which cause other theologians to reject this teaching. Rahner has provided the most satisfying response to the question why the papacy, even though it developed as an historical institution in the post-apostolic Church, is now irreversible. In keeping with his usual methodology, he begins with the present-day Church's belief that the papacy is necessary. Rahner wishes to demonstrate that this assertion does not contradict the conclusions of scriptural exegetes and historians of the early Church. On strictly historical evidence he concedes that, during the earliest period of the ancient Church, many possibilities were still open for structuring the community. The Church's hierarchical constitution, including the papacy, has a "past history, a period of development in which it came to be what it is, even though this process of becoming did not take place as a matter of logical necessity."[8] Thus Rahner holds that the papacy is irreversible even though it resulted from free historical decisions, because those decisions express the essential nature of the Church. Insofar as this particular decision is historical, he says, it cannot be undone, since it shares in the one-way direction of all historical processes. In this way Rahner defends his theory that the origin of the papacy in genuine historical decisions, guided by the Holy Spirit, is compatible with holding it to be divinely instituted and therefore an enduring structure in the Church.

Contemporary theologians are careful to avoid confusing the irreversibility of the papacy with the idea of its irreformability. The papacy, they maintain, is not immutable. Until recently, an inflationary tendency had characterized Catholic theology. Nearly everything connected with the justification and the exercise of primatial authority was thought to belong to the Church's immutable constitution. Present-day writers, however, note that in the evolution from Petrine primacy into papal primacy some developments are irreversible and others are reversible. Once this distinction is made, it appears that Christ instituted fewer irreversible elements than had formerly been taught. For many reasons, change, even considerable change, is compatible with holding to the substantial permanence of papal primacy.

In the future the Church must scrutinize closely which precise elements in the papal office are irreversible. As Rahner says, "Theologians and Popes today must give special attention to clarifying what in the doctrine and practice of the primacy of Rome really does or does not pertain to the core of belief."[9] In other words, within the papacy as an institution, it is imperative to distinguish between the unchangeable nucleus in the papal office and its embodiment in changeable forms. The majority of theologians do not see any contradiction between holding fast to the papacy as a necessary and permanent structure of the Church and at the same time calling for changes in the future exercise of papal authority.

Lutherans

On the question of the irreversibility of papal primacy and hence of its necessity to the Church, the majority of theologians and laymen uphold the classical Lutheran position: every form of ecclesial ministry, including the papacy, is optional. Even if they are willing to accept Petrine primacy and a kind of succession to that primacy in a Petrine function (a subject to be treated at length in the next chapter), they nevertheless agree with Luther and Melanchthon that the papacy is inessential to the Church. In order not to "unchurch" themselves, Lutherans reject any suggestion of the absolute necessity of papal primacy which is put forward by Catholic irreversibilists.

Although most Lutherans do not apply either the term *esse* or *bene esse* to the papacy, Paul Empie, a late member of the American Lutheran-Catholic Dialogue, raised the question using this vocabulary: "Is the papacy of the *esse* or the *bene esse* of the Church? Is it of the essence or is it just a good practice?"[10] He dismisses holding it to be essential to the Church but is willing to accept it as beneficial under certain conditions. Empie thinks that Lutherans can agree to a *bene esse* role for the papacy.

Lutheran theologians outline several reasons why the papacy is not constitutive of the Church. In the first place, such a claim to absolute necessity lacks a biblical basis. Second, many churches, including the major Protestant churches of the West, the Anglican Communion and the Orthodox churches, now exist as full ecclesial realities without being in communion with the Roman See. Furthermore, the early history of the Church provides no proof that the papacy is necessary, since an authentic ecclesial existence without the primatial office prevailed in the past when Roman claims were not universally acknowledged. Third, because the papacy is not a sacramental reality, it is therefore unnecessary for salvation. Only that which is absolutely required for salvation can belong to the Church's nature. Fourth, the Augsburg Confession excludes mention of a universal office or papacy as essential to the Church. Article 7 merely states, "It is sufficient for the true unity of the Christian Church that the Gospel be preached in conformity with a pure understanding of it and that the sacraments be administered in accordance with the divine Word." In no sense then do Lutherans recognize papal primacy as absolutely necessary to ecclesial integrity.

Papacy as Functionally Necessary

Although Lutheran theologians deny the absolute necessity of papal primacy, a few writers, including Joseph Burgess and George Lindbeck, have suggested that the papacy be considered contingently or "functionally" necessary to the Church. They think that such a functional necessity is a mediating or third-way position which could foster ecumenical dialogue between the churches. If both Lutherans and Catholics could acknowledge the papacy as functionally necessary, they say, such a formulation would satisfy the dogmatic requirements of both traditions. In other words, the papacy can be justified as appropriate (*bene esse*) but not as absolutely necessary (*esse*).

These Lutheran functionalists consider a contingently necessary papacy in the light of their traditional teaching that every concrete form of ecclesial ministry is an *adiaphoron,* something that makes no essential difference. It is a commonplace tenet among Lutheran theologians that no obligatory ecclesial structure can be deduced from the New Testament. Ecclesial organization is necessary because the Gospel must be preached in time and space, but "the specific form of church structure makes no difference as long as the form does not subvert the Gospel, unity, and Christian freedom."[11] Any ecclesial institution, therefore, which is neither demanded nor forbidden by the Word of God, is entirely optional.

Since Lutherans make no provision for ministerial structure other than preaching the Gospel and administering the sacraments, the Church is free to shape its own structure as long as it serves those ends.[12] Because Lutheran theologians recognize that *all* ecclesial institutions are *adiaphora,* they have no reason in principle to rule out the papacy as a legitimate office. Thus, the theory of a functionally necessary papacy falls squarely within the bounds of the Lutheran tradition.

Burgess and Lindbeck are willing to grant that Roman primacy developed in accordance with God's will. Nevertheless, despite this important concession, the question remains whether recognition of the papacy is required in every plan for reunion among Christians. These two theologians admit that in the past God used the papacy for the good of the Church. Given the present scandal of a divided and weakened Christendom, they recommend that Lutherans might recognize the papacy once again.

Their willingness to accept papal primacy is, however, dependent on their theory of contingent, not absolute, necessity. Not every institution God has used in the history of the Church is irreversibly necessary. As Burgess points out, "The Gospel is of course 'irreversibly necessary'; that which functions to unify God's Church for the sake of its universal mission is 'irreversibly necessary'; but from the Lutheran point of view the historical papacy is 'contingently necessary'. "[13]

Lindbeck agrees. In light of the past and looking to the future, papal primacy can be accepted as an institution which is "historically relative and conditioned." At the present time, the papacy is "the only historically available instrumentality" which can effectively carry out the necessary service of unity to the universal Church. It is functional, that is, "necessary for the sake of the Gospel." Lindbeck goes on to remark that "what is historically and functionally necessary for the welfare of the Church is also what God wills that the Church be and do."[14] The papacy then has a role in the Church by God's design. Nonetheless, it is not unconditionally required, since we have no divine guarantee that in the future it will be the papacy which will necessarily fulfill this service of unity.

Lindbeck insists, however, that this functional necessity which he recognizes involves more than merely a recommendation that the papacy be seriously considered as beneficial to the Church. Even granting that papal primacy is in principle reversible, he still thinks that it should be recognized as demanded by faith itself: "A historically and functionally (i.e., evangelically) conditioned necessity can ground moral imperatives which are no less absolute than if the necessity were also irreversible."[15] The possibility that the papacy may at some future time be set aside does not imply that it is now only optional. Lindbeck is convinced that his theory can be accepted by Catholic functionalists, including Küng and others. At the same time, he also recognizes that Catholic irreversibilists would object to his proposal on the grounds that the Pope is the necessary and permanent, not conditional, bearer of Petrine primacy in the Church.[16]

Even if the majority of Lutheran theologians disagree about the theoretical principle involved, the proposal of Burgess and Lindbeck has moved discussion on the necessity of the papacy into a new framework in which the sterile antagonism of polemical positions is now moribund.

Lutheran-Catholic Dialogue

The joint statement of American Lutherans and Catholics, *Differing Attitudes Toward Papal Primacy* (1974), contains nothing detailed on the necessity of the papacy. The statement does mention that formerly Catholics tended to think that nearly every exercise of papal primacy was divinely authorized, while they ignored the possibility for significant change, renewal or reform (#8).

In the course of the dialogue, however, the Catholic participants came to accept that just as in the past the historical forms of the papacy were adapted to changing situations, so can they now be modified to meet the needs of the Church in the future (#21). The papacy which is absolutely necessary is not, they say, to be unequivocally identified with the primatial ministry as it is currently exercised by the bishop of Rome.

For their part, the Lutheran participants frequently repeat this caveat: the papacy they are considering is not the papacy as it now exists in the Catholic Church. Accordingly, the question of the divine institution of the papal office is less of a problem than the way in which the Pope exercises his authority: "The one thing necessary, from a Lutheran point of view, is that papal primacy be so structured and interpreted that it clearly serve the Gospel and the unity of the Church of Christ, and that its exercise of power not subvert Christian freedom" (#28; cf 30, 48).

Both the Catholic and Lutheran members of the American Dialogue recognize three norms which should govern renewal in the exercise of papal authority: legitimate diversity, collegiality, and subsidiarity (#23–25). In spite of the brief descriptions of these principles for reform, the participants conclude that they have "not adequately explored to what extent the existing forms of the papal office are open to change in the future" (#30). While all members of the Dialogue share the opinion that the historical forms of the papacy are changeable, they disagree about how necessary the institution of papal primacy itself is.

Lest their refusal to entertain the necessity of the historical papacy (though not, as we shall see, of the Petrine function) be misinterpreted as indifference, the Lutheran participants include a strong plea for recognizing the ministerial function of the papacy. This need for a universal ministry, they hold, should be considered more seriously than if it were "merely optional." Indeed, "it is God's will that the Church have the institutional means needed for the promotion of unity in the Gospel" (#42). The value of an office of unity is therefore not to be dealt with simply in a casual manner. Nevertheless, Lutherans do not go beyond admitting that their teachings about the Church and its ministry allow them to believe that "recognition of papal primacy is possible to the degree that a renewed papacy would in fact foster faithfulness to the Gospel and truly exercise a Petrine function within the Church" (#48).

Unlike their Lutheran colleagues, the Catholics maintain that "acceptance of the papal office is imperative" (#49). They repeat here the irreversibilist teaching, insisting that papal primacy is an institution "in accordance with God's will" (#30). In addition, the Catholic participants cannot foresee any circumstances "that would make it desirable, even if it were possible, to abolish the papal office" (#60). In a word, the papacy should be regarded as God's "gracious gift to his people" (#21).

Commentators agree with the Dialogue participants that the question of the papacy as a constitutive element of the Church remains an unresolved problem. Catholic theologians generally support their own colleagues' clarification in the document that the papacy is necessary to the Church's constitution. Cardinal Jan Willebrands, for example, comments that the Lutheran evaluation of papal primacy as "possible and desirable" is not equivalent to Catholic teaching, since it means that according to the will of Christ the papacy is inessential to the Church.[17] Most of the Catholic critics take an irreversibilist stance and thereby support the position taken by their colleagues in the joint statement. Such a Lutheran view, though highly praised for what it does say, does not represent all that Catholics believe about the necessity of papal primacy.

Anglicans

As part of their re-evaluation of the papacy, Anglican theologians inevitably turn their attention to a question of vital importance: How is papal primacy related to the nature of the Church?

Although our study is limited to Anglicans favorably disposed to the papacy, we should not forget J. Robert Wright's salutary reminder that "not all Anglicans are yet convinced that the Church *needs* any sort of Pope or that the Gospel even allows for one."[18] Like their functionalist Lutheran colleagues, however, some Anglicans are taking another look at the need for the papacy. Anglican theologians are now applying to the papacy the terminology of *bene esse* and *plene esse,* terms which they have traditionally reserved for

discussion on the need for the episcopacy. In proposing that papal
primacy belongs either to the "well-being" (*bene esse*) or to the "fullness" (*plene esse*) of the Church, these theologians share the views of
those Lutherans who attribute a functional necessity to the papacy.
No Anglican, of course, considers the papacy to belong to the very
essence (*esse*) of the Church; that is, no Anglican believes that a community's ecclesial reality depends absolutely on communion with the
bishop of Rome.

Papacy and the Well-Being of the Church

A rather large group of contemporary Anglican theologians and
churchmen, including Arthur Allchin, Henry Chadwick, Reginald
Fuller, John Macquarrie, Eric Mascall and J. Robert Wright, have
begun to evaluate the papacy as a beneficial institution at the service
of the universal Church. Without the Pope, the one Church of Christ
is still present in a given community, but it is lacking a ministry
which could serve the effective preaching of the Gospel. The papacy,
then, can be considered a worthwhile institution, though not an exigency of the divine plan of salvation. In this understanding necessity
means something similar to the recent Lutheran theory of "functional necessity."

Anglicans first worked out the terminology of *bene esse* and
plene esse in reference to the episcopacy. At the outset they held that
the episcopacy was beneficial to the Church but not constitutive of it.
Cranmer's introduction to the Ordinal, and his view, expressed to
Henry VIII, that bishops get their authority not from God but from
the king demonstrate that the first Anglicans did not hold the episcopacy to be of divine institution. Article 36 of the Thirty-Nine Articles (1563) assumed the legitimacy of an episcopal polity but did not
regard it as necessary to the Church. Early Anglican theologians and
churchmen, therefore, regarded the episcopacy as neither divinely instituted nor necessary. At the same time, because of its traditional
importance as an ecclesial polity, it did belong to the well-being
(*bene esse*) of the Church.

The Lambeth Conferences, official and regular meetings of Anglican bishops from all over the world, have vacillated in their presentation of the necessity of the episcopacy. In 1888 the bishops

considered the episcopacy to be part of the sacred deposit of faith entrusted to the Church, but in the statement on Christian unity at the 1920 Conference they dropped the reference to the need for the historic episcopate in any plan of Church union. When the Lambeth Conference of 1930 returned to its pre-1920 position, it nonetheless did not insist upon any specific understanding of the episcopacy: "We do not require of others . . . any one particular theory or interpretation of the episcopate as a condition of union." In 1948 the same view was again ratified. Agreement on the need for the episcopacy, therefore, does not rule out diverse interpretations of the nature of the episcopacy.

When a similar line of argument is applied to papal primacy, it follows that Anglicans could accept the papacy as a necessary institution, that is, as highly recommended or desirable. Because the need for a papal ministry is not mandated by a positive expression of God's will for the Church, the necessity agreed upon is contingent or functional. Nonetheless, it is possible for Anglicans to believe in the papacy as divinely guided, and that it served the good of the Church at a particular period, without believing that it was instituted by Jesus as a permanent and absolutely necessary ecclesial structure. In such a view, both the historical establishment of the papacy and its subsequent abolition may be considered as equally providential. In short, acknowledging the emergence of papal primacy as guided by the Holy Spirit does not itself answer the question whether it is a necessary and permanent institution.

Papacy and the Fullness of the Church

In addition to those who think that the papacy would be beneficial to the Church, a few Anglicans take a further step. They emphasize to a greater extent the importance of the papacy to the universal Church and show more interest in moving the Anglican Communion toward recognizing a reformed papacy. Arthur Allchin's remark is typical in this regard: "An effective Petrine office, to sustain, encourage, coordinate and unify, is vitally needed."[19] Even more insistent is John de Satgé. Without explicitly using the term *plene esse,* he holds that "complete obedience to the Christian Gospel must include full communion with the bishop of Rome, the apostle Peter's successor."[20] For de Satgé it is not enough to commend the papacy because it is useful, as if it were an optional extra. It is a permanent ministry in the Church: "To be in communion with the visible Church that claims to be built on him [Peter] is to share fully in that unity which Jesus Christ wished to bestow."[21] As long as Anglicans are not in full communion with the Roman Catholic Church and hence with the bishop of Rome, Allchin and de Satgé maintain, something is lacking to their full ecclesial reality, to the *plene esse* of their churches.

The Caroline divines were the first Anglican theologians to introduce the term "fullness." Consequently they distinguished between what belongs to the essence of the Church (*esse*), to its well-being (*bene esse*), and to its perfection (*plene esse*). Archbishop John Bramhall (†1663) formulated a distinction which later Anglicans used to their advantage: "The mistake [unchurching non-episcopalians] proceedeth from not distinguishing between the true nature and essence of a Church, which we do readily grant them, and the integrity or perfection of a Church which we cannot grant them without swerving from the judgement of the Catholic Church."[22] If historical conditions prevented establishment of an episcopacy, this did not deprive a church of valid ministry and sacraments. The seventeenth-century divines did not want to "unchurch" the non-episcopalians on the continent, but at the same time they stressed the importance and need for the episcopacy. Implicitly Bramhall distinguished between the *esse* of the Church, the ecclesial reality common to Anglicans and Protestants (as well as to Catholics and Orthodox), and its *plene esse,* that which was necessary to the Church's perfection. If a community does not possess certain institutions—among which Bramhall included the episcopacy, and certain modern theologians would include the papacy—it lacks the perfection of the Church's fullness, of its *plene esse.*

Thus, this idea of fullness stresses the papacy as more than a merely beneficial pastoral-organizational institution. According to Anglicans who favor this description, the Church's full and developed existence, its *plene esse,* demands the papacy. Nonetheless, papal primacy is not absolutely necessary. Without communion with Rome a church may be an incomplete sacramental sign, they concede, but it is still a true ecclesial reality.

Anglican proponents of a strong doctrine on the necessity of the papacy cannot, however, insist that it belongs to the Church's *esse* for two reasons. First, the Anglican Prayer Book and the Thirty-Nine Articles exclude such an interpretation. Second, a scriptural foundation for the absolute necessity of the papacy cannot be established. On the other hand, these theologians are dissatisfied with holding that papal primacy belongs only to the *bene esse* of the Church. That designation merely suggests the possible advantages of papal primacy to the Church. It presents too weakly the real desirability of the papal office. The true need for the papacy, they say, is emphasized by holding it to belong to the fullness *(plene esse)* of the Church.

Although he has not developed his theology of the papacy at length, John Macquarrie represents those Anglicans who think that the papacy belongs to the Church's fullness. He believes that the papacy must have an important role in the future of the Church. Hence, it is counter-productive to think of abolishing the papacy or of reducing the Pope to a mere figurehead. The Pope should give dynamic leadership to Christians.[23] For Macquarrie, the primacy of the Pope is constitutive of the reunited Church of the future and so belongs to its *plene esse* which will only be achieved with reunion.

Macquarrie is not alone in this view. Other theologians, and even some churchmen, including Michael Ramsey, former archbishop of Canterbury, and Kilmer Myers, late bishop of California, are of the opinion that the Church needs the Pope to preach the Gospel and to bear witness to Christian values before the world. It is inconceivable even to imagine Christian reunion if no ministry is assigned to the bishop of Rome. Without the papacy, they say, Anglicans are missing something which they need to carry out their evangelical mission.

Among Anglicans who are now favorably disposed to the papacy, the majority hold that it belongs to the *bene esse* of the Church. It would serve the well-being of the universal Church to have a primatial office, but it is not absolutely necessary either in the present or in the future. For those Anglicans who hold that the papacy belongs to the *plene esse* of the Church, however, recognition of papal primacy is a matter of greater urgency. The reunion of Christians in the future must involve acknowledging the papacy as constitutive of the Church's institutional perfection.

Anglican-Catholic Dialogue

Universal Primacy and the Papacy

Authority in the Church I (1976) mentions that the supervision (*episcope*) of the ordained bishop in the local church is "intrinsic to the Church's structure according to the mandate given by Christ and recognized by the community" (*Authority I,* #5). Episcopal ministry is constitutive of the Church. When the members of the commission turned to the papacy, however, they were less explicit. In fact, the Venice Statement reveals the clash, albeit in an irenic way, between contemporary Catholic irreversibilist views and Anglican *bene esse* and *plene esse* views on the need for the papal ministry.

According to the Venice Statement, God's will requires both a conciliar and a primatial exercise of *episcope* on behalf of the universal Church: "If God's will for the unity in love and truth of the whole Christian community is to be fulfilled, this general pattern of the complementary primatial and conciliar aspects of *episcope* serving the *koinonia* of the churches needs to be realized at the universal level" (*Authority I,* #23). The desirability of both conciliarity and primacy at the regional level led ARCIC in 1976 to recommend the same pattern at the universal level and therefore to conclude that the Church truly needs a universal primacy, a function which is not, however, immediately to be identified with the papacy.

The call for a universal primacy made by the Venice Statement is strongly reaffirmed in *Authority in the Church II* (1981). The commission envisages a universal primacy as a "necessary link between all those exercising *episcope* within the *koinonia*" (Introduction to the Final Report, #6). But just how necessary to the Church is such a universal primacy? ARCIC holds that "full visible communion between our two churches cannot be achieved without . . . the common acceptance of a universal primacy, at one with the episcopal college in the service of the *koinonia*" (Introduction to the Final Report, #9). Visible unity between Anglicans and Catholics requires a primatial oversight along with episcopal collegiality. No united Church of the future can do without a universal primate whose "ministry modeled on the role of Peter will be a sign and safeguard of such unity" (*Authority II,* #9). Although such a position is traditional for Catholics, it involved a considerable change of attitude by the Anglican participants.

In the Windsor Statement the ARCIC members take care to point out why the Anglican tradition, without betraying itself, can support the idea of a universal primacy. "Anglicanism," they report, "has never rejected the principle and practice of primacy" (*Elucidation,* #8). In light of ecumenical dialogue, theologians have recently drawn attention to the primatial role played by the archbishop of Canterbury within the Anglican Communion. The reason for this "form of primacy arose precisely from the need for a service of unity in the faith in an expanding communion of churches" (*Elucidation,* #8). Furthermore, the Lambeth Conferences have also been ways of integrating this primatial function within Anglicanism. Primacy, then, is not alien to the Anglican tradition.

The need for a universal primate is not based on sociological exigency. Nor is it required for the Church simply because Catholics have claimed that a universal primacy has been exercised by the succession of Roman bishops. Both Anglicans and Catholics agree that "the maintenance of visible unity at the universal level includes the *episcope* of a universal primate. This is a doctrinal statement" (*Elucidation,* #8). The commission commends neither a universal primacy, nor its embodiment in the primacy of the Roman See, solely on the basis of history. Rather, such a function is "an effect of the guidance of the Holy Spirit in the Church" (*Authority II,* #13).

How is the need for universal primacy related to the papacy? After acknowledging the need for primatial *episcope* in the universal Church, the Venice Statement considers the papacy as one of its possible embodiments. This pastoral supervision has been and is carried out, in fact, by the bishop of Rome. Because God wills the end—conciliar and primatial authority exercised for the good of the universal Church—he must also will the means of accomplishing this service. In the course of history only the Roman See has ever claimed and exercised such an oversight on behalf of the whole Church. Consequently, the commission concludes: "It seems appropriate that in any future union a universal primacy such as has been described should be held by that See [Rome]" (*Authority I,* #23). ARCIC invokes God's will as requiring a universal primacy, a primacy "appropriately" held by the bishop of Rome.

Although *Authority in the Church II* refers more frequently to a universal primacy than to the primacy of the bishop of Rome, it is clear that, in light of the Venice Statement #23, the members have the papacy in mind. In this recent document the commission confirms that "a universal primacy will be needed in a reunited Church and should appropriately be the primacy of the bishop of Rome" (*Authority II*, #9). Nevertheless, for at least two reasons, the Windsor Statement does not absolutely identify the need for a universal primacy with the papacy as it now exists. First, like the Fathers at Vatican I, ARCIC does not tie Petrine succession definitively to the Roman See, though it does envisage the holder of such a primacy to be the bishop of some local church. Second, the commission wishes to avoid saying that "what has evolved historically or what is currently practiced by the Roman See is necessarily normative" (*Elucidation*, #8). With its repeated stress on conciliarity and collegiality, ARCIC wants to leave wide scope for carrying out such a universal primacy in new and different ways. Despite these reservations, the ARCIC members acknowledge the need for a universal primacy, a role which can be appropriately filled by the bishop of Rome.[24]

Papacy and Ecclesiality

According to the Venice Statement, a difficulty arises for Anglicans if the Catholic claim for the divine right of the papacy implies that "as long as a church is not in communion with the bishop of Rome, it is regarded by the Roman Catholic Church as less than fully a church" (*Authority I*, #24b). In the past Anglicans have commonly supposed, along with many Catholic theologians, that the claim to divine right for papal primacy implied denying the ecclesial reality of the churches of the Anglican Communion. If this is authentic Catholic teaching, then for Anglicans "any reconciliation with Rome would require a repudiation of their past history, life and experience—which in effect would be a betrayal of their own integrity" (*Authority II*, #14). For these reasons, then, "Roman Catholic teaching that the bishop of Rome is universal primate by divine right or law has been regarded by Anglicans as unacceptable" (*Authority II*, #15). But is this still the case?

Commentaries on the Venice Statement brought into the open

recent developments in both Anglican and Catholic theology on the extent to which being in communion with the bishop of Rome affects a church's ecclesial status. Anglican commentators were careful to point out that they could not accept papal primacy on dogmatic grounds because "such a universal primacy cannot be shown to be essential to the being of a true church."[25] At the Anglican General Synod of 1977, Bishop A. J. Trillo admitted that a "real obstacle to full agreement" remained if the Catholic members of ARCIC meant to imply that any church in the Anglican Communion is less than fully a church because it lacked communion with the Roman See.[26] Julian Charley, member of ARCIC, summed up Anglican reaction on the necessity of the papacy and its relationship to ecclesiality by recalling that "there is a world of difference between regarding the primacy of the Roman See as 'part of God's design' providentially, and holding it to be a *sine qua non* of ecclesiality and catholicity."[27]

Many Catholic critics supported their Anglican colleagues on this point: the ecclesial reality of a church does not depend on its being in communion with the bishop of Rome. These critics asked whether to lack this bond of communion with the Pope "deprives an ecclesial body of an essential mark of the Church and has fatal consequences," that is, whether the papacy is so crucial that a church without it is "simply a deceit and counterfeit, a body whose word and sacrament are robbed of all reality."[28] When the question is posed in this way Catholic critics inevitably reply that, though the papacy is necessary, its absence in a church's ministerial structure does not totally negate its authentic ecclesiality.

These critical views influenced ARCIC's later formulation in the Windsor Statement. To hold that the papacy is of divine right does not thereby "unchurch" the Anglican Communion. "The doctrine that a universal primacy expresses the will of God," says the Windsor Statement, "does not entail the consequence that a Christian community out of communion with the See of Rome does not belong to the Church of God" (*Authority II,* #12). According to ARCIC, disastrous ecclesial consequences do not therefore follow from the Catholic claim for the divine right of the papacy.

Authority in the Church II presents its understanding of the relationship between papacy and ecclesiality. The commission members note that the Catholic Church recognizes the Orthodox churches as true ecclesial realities despite their rejection of papal primacy. Furthermore, according to the ecclesiology of Vatican II, the Church of Christ is not co-extensive with the Catholic Church nor exclusively embodied in it (*Authority II,* #12). God's design for a universal primacy appropriately held by the bishop of Rome does not imply therefore that the churches of the Anglican Communion are not already churches.

Some Catholic critics of the Venice Statement did specifically link acceptance of papal primacy with a particular church's *full* ecclesiality. Bishop Christopher Butler, for example, a Catholic member of ARCIC, thought that the statement should have spoken more explicitly of Rome as "the obligatory center of communion" in the Church. Visible ecclesial unity, manifested through communion with the Roman See, is not just an optional extra; it is required out of obedience to Christ's will.[29] Moreover, many Anglican theologians who see papal primacy as belonging to the fullness of the Church, to its *plene esse,* would agree with Butler. Without explicitly dealing with this question, the Windsor Statement does however suggest that something is lacking to the churches of the Anglican Communion because they do not belong to "the visible manifestation of full Christian communion which is maintained in the Roman Catholic Church" (*Authority II,* #12). Even though not all Anglicans and Catholics may agree on precisely how necessary the papacy is to the Church, the Final Report of ARCIC is certainly a testimony to the need for a primatial *episcope,* embodied in the papacy, to be at the service of the universal communion of churches.

Notes

1. "Nicht mitherrschen, sondern mitdienen," in *Papsttum-heute und morgen,* ed. Georg Denzler (Regensburg, 1975) 71.

2. Dulles, "*Ius Divinum* as an Ecumenical Problem," 703–704.

3. *Why We Need the Pope,* 120–123, 137.

4. *The Church,* 409–413; *On Being a Christian,* 491.

5. *The Church,* 476; *On Being a Christian,* 500.

6. "*Ius Divinum* as an Ecumenical Problem," 702.

7. *Papacy in Transition,* 3.

8. "Basic Observations on the Subject of Changeable and Unchangeable Factors in the Church," in *Theological Investigations* 14 (New York, 1976) 17.

9. "Open Questions in Dogma Considered by the Institutional Church as Definitively Answered," *Journal of Ecumenical Studies* 15 (1978) 218.

10. *Lutherans and Catholics in Dialogue: Personal Notes for a Study* (Philadelphia, 1981) 120.

11. Burgess, "Lutherans and Papacy," 37.

12. Lindbeck, "The Lutheran Doctrine of the Ministry: Catholic and Reformed," *Theological Studies* 30 (1969) 592.

13. "Lutherans and Papacy," 32.

14. "Papacy and *Ius Divinum*: A Lutheran View," in *Papal Primacy and the Universal Church*, 199–203.

15. *Ibid.*, 205.

16. *Ibid.*, 200–208.

17. "Roman Catholic/Lutheran Dialogue in the U.S.A.—Papal Primacy: An Appraisal," *One in Christ* 13 (1977) 216.

18. "Anglicans and Papacy," 205.

19. "Can a Petrine Office Be Meaningful in the Church? An Anglican Reply," in *Papal Ministry in the Church*, 130.

20. *Peter and the Single Church*, ix.

21. *Ibid.*, 156.

22. *Vindication of Himself and the Episcopal Clergy from the Presbyterian Charge of Popery*, in *The Works of John Bramhall*, ed. A. W. Haddan (Oxford, 1844) 3, 518.

23. *Christian Unity and Christian Diversity* (London, 1975) 99.

24. David Miles Board, *Authority in the Church: A Guide* (n.p., n.d.) 15–16.

25. McAdoo, *Being an Anglican*, 48.

26. *Report of the Proceedings: General Synod* (London, 1977) 343.

27. *Agreement on Authority: The Anglican-Roman Catholic Statement with Commentary* (Bramcote, 1977) 25.

28. *Truth and Authority*, 25–26.

29. "Authority in the Church," *Tablet* 231 (1977) 479–480.

5
Petrine Function and Papacy

The term "Petrine function" was first introduced into ecumenical discussion on the papacy by Lutherans and has now been adopted in some form or other by Anglicans and Catholics. It refers to that ministry which derives from and now embodies the role and responsibility in the apostolic college which Peter rendered to the founding generation of the Church. The term allows ecumenists to study possible solutions to the stalemate which inevitably arises concerning the relationship between Petrine primacy and succession to that primacy.

The concept associates the New Testament ministry of Peter with the papacy, without, however, necessarily claiming that the Pope is the historical successor of Peter. Catholics indeed do believe in such a succession, but Lutherans and Anglicans are generally a good deal less convinced. Some non-Catholics relate the Petrine function to the papacy; others do not. Though use of this term offers no simple solution to theological questions, it does allow us to recognize the growing consensus which theologians are reaching and to identify the precise problems which remain for future ecumenical discussion.

In *Differing Attitudes Toward Papal Primacy* (1974), the participants in the American Lutheran-Catholic Dialogue refer to the Petrine function as "a particular form of ministry exercised by a person, officeholder, or local church with reference to the Church as a whole"; it also "serves to promote and preserve the oneness of the

Church by symbolizing unity, and by facilitating communication, mutual assistance or correction, and collaboration in the Church's mission" (#4).

What is at the origin of the Petrine function? Some Lutherans and Anglicans have no difficulty, as we have seen in Chapter 2, in accepting that Peter fulfilled a unique role in the apostolic Church— what Catholic theology traditionally calls Petrine primacy. Indeed, some Lutherans interpret the Petrine texts to mean that Peter received this responsibility from Jesus himself. Other Lutherans, however, trace the origins of this function to the apostolic community. In the same way, some Anglican theologians, but not all, also admit that there is a scriptural, and possibly even a dominical, basis for a Petrine function.

Is the Petrine function still alive in the Church? Theologians use this term or its equivalent to differentiate the permanence of that ministry given to Peter, with whatever it entails, from the historical papacy. Lutherans can thereby affirm the permanence of a Petrine function in the Church, without at the same time having to identify this ministry with papal primacy. Anglican theologians are similarly disposed to admit the possibility of succession to a Petrine function in the Church as long as they do not have to equate this Petrine ministry unequivocally with the papacy. As for most Catholics, they have no doubt about the permanence of a Petrine office and identify it with papal primacy. Consequently, theologians from the three traditions can all agree that there is a Petrine function willed by Jesus. They do not agree, however, on how this ministry ought to continue in the Church.

The possibility of making a theological distinction between a Petrine function instituted by Christ and its historical form, always an *adiaphoron,* has opened the way for ecumenically-minded Lutherans to reconsider their attitude to the need for a universal ministry. Their increasing awareness of the Church's universal dimension had led them to appreciate the value of a ministerial office dedicated to the preservation and promotion of unity among the various local churches.

In the American Lutheran-Catholic Dialogue, the Lutheran participants accepted that the Petrine function is desirable, even if not demanded by the Gospel. The worldwide mission of the Church would greatly benefit from such a unifying ministry. In the introduction to *Differing Attitudes Toward Papal Primacy,* the participants observe that "there is a growing awareness among Lutherans of the necessity of a specific ministry to serve the Church's unity and universal mission." This need for a universal ministry should be considered, according to the Lutheran members, as more than "merely optional." Indeed, "it is God's will that the Church have the institutional means needed for the promotion of unity in the Gospel" (#42).

At the same time Lutheran theologians note that their present ecclesial structures do not adequately provide for such a ministry. This lack is increasingly experienced as a disadvantage for the effective preaching of the Gospel in the modern world. At the local level, to be sure, the pastor does act in this capacity, but at the universal level there is no corresponding ministry. Just as the need for unity within the local church led to a Lutheran re-evaluation of the episcopal office, so also the same need within the universal Church, comments Wolfhart Pannenberg, demonstrates "the desirability and perhaps even the necessity" of an office dedicated to the preservation of unity.[1]

Some Anglican theologians, such as Henry Chadwick, John Macquarrie, Eric Mascall and John de Satgé, have likewise recognized the need for a primatial office, though not necessarily the papacy, which would promote and preserve the unity of the Church and its faith. Bishop John Moorman affirms this need for a center of unity in the Church to be "absolutely indispensable."[2]

In addition to preserving the unity of the Church, Lutheran and Anglican theologians recognize another task fulfilled by the Petrine function: it provides a ministry of authoritative teaching for the edification of all the churches. The faithful preaching of the Gospel to the modern world requires an office dedicated to this goal, a ministry which can be identified with the Lord's commission to Peter.[3] The Petrine function, which is permanent, should carry out this leadership responsibility.

Who Carries Out the Petrine Function Today?

1. Catholic Views

Catholic theologians generally introduce the Petrine function-historical papacy distinction into their theology in order to clarify the limits of reform possible in the Pope's exercise of his primatial authority. The majority of theologians use the distinction to draw attention to the many different ways in which the Petrine function has been realized by the Church in the past and thereby conclude that reforms can be contemplated for the future. They affirm the necessity of an historical realization of the Petrine function in the papacy, without absolutizing any one particular form it has taken over the centuries. By studying the different ways in which the Pope has exercised his ministry, a theologian can separate the changeable from the unchangeable, or the reversible from the irreversible, in the Petrine function.

Undoubtedly the mainstream of Catholic theologians believe that the successor of St. Peter, whom tradition has designated to be the bishop of Rome, exercises the Petrine function for the good of the Church and according to God's will. The papacy, they say, must be in historical continuity with the ministry Jesus conferred on Peter.

The Catholic members of the American Lutheran-Catholic Dialogue, for instance, insist that within the episcopal college the Pope personally succeeds to the role Peter fulfilled in the apostolic college (#53). In spite of the human failings of some Popes, the papacy has been a "signal help in protecting the Gospel and the Church against particularistic distortions" (#60). For Catholics, the Petrine function has been "entrusted by the will of Christ" to the bishop of Rome (#29); it will continue to be his charge in the future. No office could ever replace the papacy. Such are the irreversibilist views of the Catholic members of the Dialogue and of most other Catholic theologians as well.

Functionalist theologians, however, consider the papacy to be merely *one* legitimate form of the Petrine function which developed due to historical contingencies. The papacy, as Karl-Heinz Ohlig says, is not the exclusive bearer of this ministry: "It can no longer be maintained theologically that the Roman primacy is the only Chris-

tian form possible for the office of unity."[4] According to the functionalists, therefore, the papal form of the Petrine ministry is, at least
in principle, reversible and temporary.

An important clarification must, however, be made. Those
Catholic theologians who would substitute another office or offices
for the papacy are to be distinguished from those who would concede
that the present papal embodiment of the Petrine function can be
complemented by other structures. Only the most radical functionalists assert that in theory the papacy could be replaced. According to
Paul Misner, for example, the ministry of unity now fulfilled by the
papacy could be carried out by the episcopal college even without the
Pope.[5] But, in fact, the functionalists' stance is more moderate. Even
Ohlig, for whom the development of totally new forms of the Petrine
ministry is theologically admissible, grants on practical and historical grounds that papal primacy should not be abolished.[6]

Karl Rahner and Avery Dulles are among those theologians
who suggest radically new ways of exercising Petrine authority. Unlike the functionalists, however, they do not divorce new forms of the
Petrine ministry from its historical institutionalization in the papacy.
Both have suggested a kind of "shared papacy" which could carry
out the taxing burden of the Petrine function more effectively than a
single individual.

Rahner maintains that we should distinguish between an individual person and a moral person as a holder of apostolic authority.
In the case of the episcopacy, for instance, the legitimate exercise of
episcopal authority in a local church can exist apart from its embodiment in a single bishop who is head of the community. What is demanded by divine law is simply the presence in the local ecclesial
community of apostolic authority. Therefore, it is theoretically possible that a small group of persons or a central body, and not only a
monarchical bishop, might possess this episcopal authority.[7] Later
Rahner applies the same argument to papal primacy. In this case, the
Petrine function would have to be permanently present in the universal Church but it would not necessarily have to be exercised by a single individual, the Pope.[8] Dulles makes the same point as Rahner:
"In theory, the Petrine function could be performed either by a single individual presiding over the whole Church or by some kind of

committee, board, synod or parliament—possibly with a 'division of powers' into judicial, legislative, administrative and the like.'"[9]

Many Catholics, however, including Yves Congar, Walter Kasper, Joseph Ratzinger and Leo Scheffczyk, have expressed serious reservations about such a separation of the Petrine function from the historical papacy. They focus their objections on the danger of the unhistorical and unincarnational understanding of revelation which could result. The Petrine function cannot simply be separated from the bishop of Rome as a chemist might separate one element from a compound. These theologians base their objection on the very nature of revelation. The Lord does not reveal himself in abstract principles or by instituting depersonalized structures. Rather, God's will is made known through his dealings with humanity. Moreover, the Petrine function-historical papacy distinction is fraught with problems. To distinguish the Petrine function in so radical a way from papal primacy is contrary to the Catholic tradition. While Catholics can be open to the possibility of reforming papal structures, the idea of a "shared papacy" represents the views of only a few scholars.

Catholic theologians generally concede, of course, that no absolute identity exists between the present shape of the papacy and the Petrine ministry. In varying degrees some accept that the Petrine function can be shared with, but not replaced by, other bodies such as a permanent synod or the episcopal college. In theory, then, there could be multiple successors to the Petrine function. But the majority still insist that there is a primatial Petrine authority which can be exercised only by the bishop who is recognized as the successor of St. Peter. They reserve a preeminent role for the Pope; without him, they say, the fullness of the Petrine ministry would not be present in the Church.

2. Lutheran Views

The very fact that Lutheran theologians make use of the Petrine function-historical papacy distinction proves that they are reinterpreting their traditional rejection of papal primacy. According to this revisionist view, the sixteenth-century reformers set aside the papacy only conditionally, insofar as it was an unworthy and corrupt institutionalization of the Petrine function. They did not reject it absolutely, insofar as it represented a legitimate ecclesial ministry. In principle, Lutherans are not at all confessionally committed to dismissing the Petrine ministry as incompatible with Lutheran orthodoxy.

In the same way, many contemporary Lutherans now distinguish between the present-day papacy and the scripturally based Petrine function. Because they separate the more abstract Petrine ministry from the historical papacy, Lutheran theologians can enter into ecumenical dialogue on the need for a ministry of unity at the service of the universal Church.

Those who recognize the need for a Petrine function point out how the Lutheran churches are already carrying it out in practice, often even without adverting to it. In the history of the Church the Petrine office has been fulfilled in a variety of ways: by ecumenical and local councils, by theological schools, and even by the bishop of Rome.[10] At present, the Lutheran World Federation and synods, at which all the local churches are represented, exercise a kind of Petrine ministry.

However, such embodiments of a living Petrine function within Lutheranism are judged to be only partially successful. Many Lutherans have become aware of the limitations of their ecclesiastical structures. The German authors of the *Evangelical Adult Catechism* (1975) strongly regret that the Lutheran churches have been unable to express the unity of the Church in a visible form through ministries at their disposal. Consequently, they are open to the papacy as one of the ways of realizing a ministry of unity on behalf of the universal Church. According to the participants of the American Lutheran-Catholic Dialogue, Lutherans would therefore be unwise to overlook "the papacy's possible role as a symbol and center of unity of the Church universal" (#36). If the Pope's office is reformed and renewed under the Gospel, many Lutherans would then have no reason to oppose it as contrary to their tradition.

But at the same time the Petrine function is not to be identified only with the office of the Pope. History testifies to its having been filled by bishops, patriarchs and church presidents. The statement *Differing Attitudes Toward Papal Primacy* does concede, however, that in terms of duration and geographical area of responsibility the bishop of Rome has been the "single most notable representative" of this Petrine ministry (#5). Relying on their theological tradition, the Lutheran participants in the American Dialogue state: "There is for Lutherans no single or uniquely legitimate form of the exercise of the Petrine function. At every stage, the Petrine function developed according to the possibilities available at that time" (#41). In the International Roman Catholic-Lutheran Commission's report, *Ways to Community* (1980), the participants likewise recognize that "a ministry serving the unity of the Church as a whole is, for Lutherans, in accord with the will of the Lord, but without its concrete form having been fixed once and for all" (#23). A reformed papal form of the Petrine office would be acceptable under certain conditions, but it is not a constitutive element of the Church.

Nor do the Lutheran members of the Dialogue hold the present papal office to be the optimal way of fulfilling the need for a ministry of unity. They state quite clearly, "The best model for the exercise of the Petrine function through a papacy is an issue that remains to be determined" (#46). At most, a renewed and reformed papacy would provide an opportunity for carrying out a ministry of unity on behalf of the universal Church.

It is, therefore, entirely acceptable for a Lutheran to hold that the Petrine function is essential to the Church without making a similar affirmation for the papacy. Peter Meinhold, for example, maintains that by definition the realization of the Petrine ministry demands a charism, a free gift of the Spirit. But it is possible that a given Pope may not have such a charism for directing the Church. Since this free gift is not irrevocably bound to the papacy as an office, the Church has no guarantee that the bishop of Rome will always be the one who will carry out the Petrine function.[11] Ultimately, what the Church requires as a *sine qua non* is the presence of the Petrine charism in some form or other and not the historical papacy. At times, however, and the present may very well be one of those periods, the bishop of Rome does have the Petrine charism and so can fulfill the ministry of unity. For this reason, many Lutherans are prepared to consider the papacy as an authentic ministry in the Church. Nonetheless, it is possible that in the future some office other than the papacy could carry out this function more effectively and without being in continuity with the bishop of Rome.

Other Lutherans, such as Reinhard Frieling and Werner Ritter, believe that the Church should not limit the embodiment of the Petrine function to one personal successor at any given time. The multiple charisms from the New Testament which are attributed to the apostle—Peter as rock, keeper of the keys, strengthener, pastor, etc.—should not continue to be concentrated exclusively in one person or even in one institution. Rather, the possibility ought to be left open to carry out the scripturally based Petrine function in various ways.[12]

3. Anglican Views

The introduction of the distinction between the Petrine function and papal primacy as a way of dealing with ecumenical questions on the papacy has not taken hold among historically-minded Anglicans to the same extent as it has among Lutherans. When Anglican theologians refer to the Petrine charge inherited by the whole Church, they are making a clear distinction between the Petrine ministry and the papacy. Although it was Peter who first personally carried out this ministry at the Lord's bidding, its later embodiments are by no means limited to the bishop of Rome. Every bishop in the universal Church fulfills in his own way the Petrine function of unifying his local church. In a sense, then, the episcopal college is responsible for carrying out the Petrine mission of leading and teaching, a function which Catholics traditionally associate with the papacy.

Although Anglicans do not unequivocally identify this Petrine ministry with the bishop of Rome, some of them are more open than Lutherans to the idea that the Pope *should* be the holder of this ministry within a reunited Church. On historical and practical grounds, they argue, the papacy is the only institution which can make a serious claim to embody Petrine authority. In a draft document at the Lambeth Conference of 1968, the bishops recognized the need for a president within the episcopal college and admitted that "this president might most fittingly be the occupant of the historic See of Rome." In a 1970 meeting in Venice, the Anglican participants of the Anglican-Roman Catholic International Commission agreed that the papacy could be justified as a legitimate historical development of Jesus' commission to Peter. As the papacy had been a valuable sign in the past of the unity of the Church, so might it carry out such a mission again in the future.

Many Anglican theologians believe that it would be unhistorical and untraditional to invent new ways of fulfilling the Petrine function, since the bishop of Rome can be recognized as appropriately carrying out that role. Nonetheless, most insist on a reform in the Catholic understanding and exercise of this function before reunion can occur. Edward Yarnold points out how ARCIC attached the Petrine function to the papacy more firmly than the American Lutheran-Catholic Dialogue was willing to do. The commission views the Church primarily as a community which requires the leadership of the ordained ministry at both the local and the universal level. After citing #23 of *Authority in the Church I* (1976), Yarnold comments that even the Anglican participants envisaged that "the Petrine ministry needs to be exercised by a single person, whose authority is balanced by a college of co-responsible sharers."[13] The justification for such a ministry is the scripturally based tradition of the two churches and the Anglican saying that "a committee cannot be a father in God."

According to John de Satgé, the present ecumenical climate makes it impossible to ignore the Catholic claim that the Petrine ministry is embodied in the Pope. He thinks that the recent developments in the exercise of the ministry of the bishop of Rome make it clear that only the Pope can fulfill the Petrine function: "One service of especial importance to the modern world can be given only to the papacy: a center of religious authority which is at once universal and personal."[14]

In the Windsor Statement (1981), the members of ARCIC make a single reference to a "Petrine function and office" (#32). Unlike the Venice Statement which refers only to a universal primacy, *Authority in the Church II* is replete with references to a personally exercised *episcope* of what *The Times* of London has called "the vaguely Darwinian figure of a universal primate." ARCIC agrees that the continuity between Peter's ministry and the Pope's is "not contrary to the New Testament" (*Authority II,* #7), but is also careful to distinguish this Petrine function from the present papacy. The statement studiously avoids exclusively identifying the universal primate with the Pope. It is clear, moreover, that the primacy referred to is not that "as it now exists in its purely Roman Catholic context," as Bishop Henry McAdoo, Anglican co-chairman of ARCIC remarks, "but as it should be in the context of a united Church."[15] In other words, the Windsor Statement provides a vision and promise of how a universal primate should exercise his authority rather than a description of present Roman practice. ARCIC uses this valuable distinction to promote its view that the bishop of Rome is an appropriate holder of a Petrine ministry which is open to reform in light of the ideal presented of a universal primate.

Despite the drawbacks of the Petrine function-historical papacy distinction, many Anglican, Lutheran and Catholic theologians have found it to be a positive contribution to ecumenical discussion on papal primacy. In the present stage of the Church's life, they agree, the Pope can authentically, if not exclusively, fulfill Peter's function for the good of the Church.

Notes

1. *Ethik und Ekklesiologie* (Göttingen, 1977) 220.

2. "Genesi e contenuto dei tre documenti pubblicati dalla Commissione Internazionale Anglicano-Cattolica Romana," *Oikumenikon* 17 (1977) 147.

3. Heinrich Ott, "Can a Petrine Office Be Meaningful in the Church? A Protestant Reply," in *Papal Ministry in the Church,* 138.

4. *Why We Need the Pope,* 122.

5. "The Papacy: Three Schools of Thought," *The Ecumenist* 11 (1973) 54.

6. Ohlig, *Why We Need the Pope,* 137.

7. "Open Questions in Dogma," 215–216.

8. *Vorfragen zu einem ökumenischen Amtsverständnis,* Quaestiones Disputatae 65 (Freiburg, 1975) 25–32.

9. "Papal Authority in Roman Catholicism," in *A Pope for All Christians?* 55.

10. Ott, "Can a Petrine Office Be Meaningful?" 132.

11. "Das Amt der Einheit—biblische, historische und ökumen-

ische Perspektiven," *Bausteine für die Einheit der Christen* 59 (1975) 22.

12. Werner H. Ritter, "Anerkennung des Papstes als evangelisch? Kritische Marginalien zu einer lutherisch-katholischen Ökumene," *Catholica* 32 (1978) 147, 156–157.

13. "The Papacy," *The Way* 19 (1979) 224.

14. *Peter and the Single Church,* 151.

15. *Church Times* (April 2, 1982) 1.

6
Where Do We Go From Here?

Although recent theology and official ecumenical dialogues have dramatically dissipated traditional polemics on papal primacy, they have not yet reached a full consensus on its origin and necessity. Must the papacy, though, remain an insurmountable obstacle to the reunion of Christians?

I suggest that at least part of the solution lies in our theological terminology. Ecumenical discussion is teaching us that a precise terminology can clarify, if not totally resolve, many of the problems which arise in a theology of the papacy. An accurate vocabulary not only lays bare the deficiencies of earlier interpretations but also defines remaining difficulties more specifically. It is time, therefore, to adopt a new terminology which better reflects the current state of agreement and disagreement on papal primacy.

Proposal for a New Terminology

In the past, when theologians held a structure or a practice to be of divine institution, they usually thought that it had been directly and immediately instituted by Jesus Christ himself. Most contemporary Catholic theologians, however, along with many Lutheran and Anglican scholars, consider an ecclesial structure to be "divinely instituted" as long as it emerged under God's direct providential guidance, even though free human decisions played a significant role in shaping it. Because of this broader interpretation, which is gaining ground among theologians and churchmen, ambiguity can now arise when the traditional vocabulary of "divine right" or "divine institution" is used for a ministerial structure such as the papacy.

From our study of recent ecumenical theology and bilateral dialogues, we can conclude that the designation "by divine institution" (*ex institutione divina*) should now be applied to an ecclesial structure only when one wishes to make a precise affirmation about its origin. By using this term, therefore, a theologian chooses to emphasize the direct and immediate intervention of the historical Jesus at the origin of such a structure. Historical factors, though always necessarily present, are secondary considerations. When a writer wishes to emphasize that a structure derives from the divine will and also that the community and contingent historical factors played a formative role in determining its shape, he should use the term "by divine design" (*ex ordinatione divina*) and not "by divine institution."

Although the principle of distinguishing between divine institution and divine design is already well established in Catholic theology, it has not been used in a theology of the papacy. Theologians and the magisterium have traditionally distinguished, for example, between the divine institution of the apostolic ministry and the divine design or divine ordination of its threefold division into bishop, priest and deacon. Christ himself directly instituted the pastoral ministry, but the apostolic Church determined its particular gradations, a development which Catholic theologians now hold to have been providentially guided and therefore irreversible.

How does this affect the papacy? Catholics have customarily used the terms "by divine right" and "by divine institution" to describe both Petrine and papal primacy. Since recent exegetical and historical studies strongly suggest that the papacy, as an operative and recognized ecclesial institution, did not emerge until the middle or the end of the second century, do we therefore conclude that the papacy should no longer be held as divinely instituted because it cannot be traced back to the explicit will of the historical Jesus?

The application of the distinction between divine institution and divine design provides an answer to this question. The Petrine function is of divine institution (*ex institutione divina*) and its embodiment in the historical papacy is of divine design (*ex ordinatione*

divina). Hence, I propose that the term divine institution be retained
to describe the origin of Petrine primacy or the Petrine function but
should be dropped to describe the origin of papal primacy.

Building on the converging opinions of recent theological discussion on the papacy, we shall now examine how ecumenical dialogue can benefit from introducing this distinction between divine
institution and divine design.

"Divine Institution" of the Petrine Function

When theologians affirm the Petrine function to be of divine institution they maintain that Christ himself instituted this ministry as
a permanent element of the Church. As we have seen, nearly all
Catholic theologians, as well as an increasing number of Lutherans
and Anglicans, accept a scriptural basis for the dominical institution
of the Petrine function.

Catholics now frequently distinguish the divinely instituted Petrine ministry from the historical papacy. They differentiate between
the permanent nucleus of the ministry that Christ established and its
historical and changeable realizations which emerged under the
guidance of the Spirit. By using scripturally based criteria, theologians can evaluate how the papal embodiment is in fact carrying out
the mission Christ entrusted to Peter. They are therefore able to propose changes in the manner of exercising primatial authority without
calling into question the legitimacy of its existence.

To an even greater extent than their Catholic colleagues, Lutherans find this separation of the Petrine function from the papacy
to be helpful: it raises the question of papal primacy in a context fully
compatible with their traditional understanding of ecclesial polity.
The early Lutherans rejected the papacy they knew, not the ministry
of unity that Jesus willed for the universal Church. Consequently, a
ministerial office serving the unity of the universal Church can be
considered legitimate. Such a ministry is a contemporary institutionalization of the function Jesus assigned to Peter in the apostolic community. Christ's promise to Peter assures the permanence of the
charism necessary for fulfilling this ministry. Even though there is no
dominical guarantee that the Petrine function must coincide with the
office of the bishop of Rome, an orthodox Lutheran can now hold

that a permanent Petrine function is desirable as an ecclesial ministry.

Because the Anglicans' approach to questions of ecclesial polity is more historical than that of the Lutherans, they make little use of the concept of a Petrine function which can be separated from the historical papacy. Still, Anglican theologians do admit that a universal primacy is in accordance with God's design for the Church. While they do not generally attribute the origin of this ministry to the historical Jesus, it is nonetheless very similar to the Petrine function, and some Anglican theologians, as well as the Windsor Statement, relate it to Peter's role in the New Testament.

"Divine Design" of Papal Primacy

Until very recently Catholic theologians taught that because the historical Jesus instituted papal primacy, it was of divine, that is, dominical, origin. Contemporary ecumenical dialogue, however, has given rise to a greater appreciation of divine providence guiding the emergence of ecclesial institutions. In this view, the papacy appeared in history when the Christian community needed a personal embodiment of the Petrine function. To a great extent, the historical papacy owes its origin to the contingencies of time, place and other circumstances dependent upon free human decisions. But Catholics also think that papal primacy developed in response to the Holy Spirit's guidance of the Church which called for incarnating the ministry Jesus conferred on Peter. Thus, the papacy is more accurately held to exist by divine design (*ex ordinatione divina*) rather than by immediate divine institution.

Catholic, Lutheran and Anglican theologians can all accept that papal primacy exists by divine design. The term affirms that the papacy's origins are a positive expression of the divine will revealed through the Spirit's guidance of the Church. At the same time, the papacy is also an ecclesial institution shaped by multiple historical, cultural and sociological influences. Papal primacy is a product of both the divine will and of truly free human decisions. A papacy held to be of divine design corresponds, therefore, to each church's beliefs about the papacy's origins. Lutherans and Anglicans emphasize the human factors, while their Catholic colleagues emphasize the divine factors. In bilateral dialogues, neither side denies what the other side stresses.

At least two advantages accrue when papal primacy is held to exist by divine design rather than by divine institution. First, this term eliminates the idea of the papacy as an absolutely immutable structure, an idea which inevitably accompanies the more traditional designation. To acknowledge the papacy as God's design for the Church avoids the impression of an institution determined once and for all in the past. Considerable room is left open for development in the way that the Pope will fulfill the Petrine function in the future. The papacy, then, is clearly an institution whose historical shape is changeable; primatial authority can be adapted to meet the needs of the Church as they will arise tomorrow.

Second, this new terminology allows theologians to pinpoint precisely where their respective interpretations of the papacy agree and disagree. When Lutherans and Anglicans admit that the papacy is a providential development in the life of the Church, they abandon their traditional position that it is only a human institution. Catholics, moreover, now acknowledge that free human decisions determined when and how the papacy finally emerged as an historical institution. Thus, in light of these positions, the question of the papacy's "divine" origin can in fact be resolved. This growing consensus is reflected by the common acceptance of the divine design of papal primacy. The significance of this agreement should not be minimized.

The remaining unresolved questions on the papacy focus on the ecclesiological consequences of holding it to be of divine design. The Catholic tradition, considering the papacy to be a constitutive element of the Church, has generally taken its necessity and irreversibility for granted. By this theologians mean that the papacy cannot be abolished or so modified that it becomes a different institution. Only very recently have a few Catholic theologians, the functionalists, suggested that the papacy is just a human institution and therefore reversible in principle. The vast majority, the irreversibilists, still hold it to be an absolutely necessary ecclesial structure which will endure as long as the Church itself. Consequently, a church not in communion with the bishop of Rome lacks the institutional fullness that it should possess.

Catholics generally believe that because the papacy is God's will for his Church, it is even now a necessary embodiment of the Petrine function. For them the papal ministry is a constitutive element of the universal Church. It is a moot point among theologians, however, whether a particular church presently not in communion with the Roman See is for that reason alone lacking full ecclesial reality.

Lutheran theologians can accept the divine design of papal primacy by emphasizing the role of human factors in its emergence as a concrete realization of God's will. Even though Lutherans do not identify the Petrine function exclusively with the papacy, the mere fact that they can consider papal primacy as a legitimate and even providential ministry is remarkable. Such a view would have been unthinkable before the Second Vatican Council. At the same time, however, were Lutherans to acknowledge a papacy by divine design, they would not thereby hold it to be an absolutely constitutive element of the Church. This difference between a Catholic and a Lutheran theology of the papacy remains unresolved and is not overcome by adopting the same term to describe papal primacy.

By accepting the divine design of the papacy Anglicans would not call into question the ecclesial reality of their churches. God indeed wills that in the reunited Church of the future a universal primacy can appropriately be held by the bishop of Rome. Even though Anglicans have been out of communion with the Pope for centuries, they do not take this to mean that God's design is indifferent to such communion. Rather, serious historical reasons have impeded its realization. Should these impediments cease to exist, then some contemporary Anglicans would accept that by God's design communion with the Roman See would be necessary for ecclesial integrity. The agreement between Anglicans and Catholics on the divine design of papal primacy would not conceal, but rather highlight, the unresolved difficulty of how each tradition regards the necessity of the papacy. According to Catholic theologians, God's design calls for the Petrine function to be exercised by a bishop who is designated as the successor of Peter. Anglicans, for the most part, do not yet agree that the papacy is a constitutive element of the Church, though if the Windsor Statement is any indication, they are rapidly moving in that direction.

Ecumenical dialogue on the papacy has come a long way in recent years. Major theological problems concerning the origin of papal primacy are being resolved. Other difficulties still remain for future dialogues. Without doubt, however, the possibility for future Christian reunion in which the bishop of Rome would be a visible sign and guarantee of unity is closer now than at any time in the last four hundred years. An increasing number of Lutherans and Anglicans accept the papacy to be in accordance with God's design for his Church.

Selected Bibliography

This list is limited to material readily available in English.

Anglican-Roman Catholic International Commission. *The Final Report*. Washington: U.S. Catholic Conference, 1982.
Contains *Authority in the Church I* (1976), *Authority in the Church: Elucidation* (1981) and *Authority in the Church II* (1981), as well as an important preface, introduction and conclusion to the deliberations of ARCIC. Fundamental documentation for Anglican-Catholic ecumenical discussion on the papacy.

Balthasar, Hans Urs von. *The Anti-Roman Attitude*. San Francisco: Ignatius, 1983.
An excellent meditative study of the biblical foundation and theological value of the papacy in the mystery of the Church.

Brown, Raymond E., Donfried, Karl P., and Reumann, John, eds. *Peter in the New Testament*. Minneapolis: Augsburg, 1973; New York: Paulist, 1973.
Sponsored by the American Lutheran-Catholic Dialogue to provide a scriptural background for ecumenical discussions on the role of the papacy in the universal Church. An up-to-date presentation of the Petrine texts and their interpretation by contemporary critical scholars of both traditions.

Dulles, Avery. "The Papacy: Bond or Barrier?" *Catholic Mind* 1285 (1974) 45–49.
Commentary on the American Lutheran-Catholic Dialogue, *Papal Primacy and the Universal Church,* by a Catholic participant favorable to its conclusions.

Dumont, Christophe. "Agreed Statement: A Critique and Analysis." *Origins* 6 (January 27, 1977) 509–515.
A favorable but cautious commentary on the Venice Statement prepared by a consultant of the Secretariat for Promoting Christian Unity who was not a member of ARCIC. Though not "official," it was published in *L'Osservatore Romano* along with *Authority in the Church I* (Venice Statement).

Empie, Paul C., and Murphy, T. Austin, eds. *Papal Primacy and the Universal Church: Lutherans and Catholics in Dialogue 5.* Minneapolis: Augsburg, 1974.
Contains both the official joint statement of the Dialogue and important essays by participants. It is the most significant ecumenical statement on the papacy yet published by Catholics and Lutherans.

Granfield, Patrick. *The Papacy in Transition.* Garden City: Doubleday, 1980.
A comprehensive summary of recent Catholic and non-Catholic work on papal primacy, with attention paid to discovering the essentials of the Petrine ministry, the historical development of the papacy, possible reforms of the office and ecumenical discussion on the role of the Pope.

Küng, Hans. *The Church.* New York: Sheed & Ward, 1967.
Contains the essentials of Küng's controversial presentation of the origins and function of the papal ministry with his preference for a primacy of pastoral service, not of jurisdiction (pp. 444–480).

Küng, Hans, ed. *Papal Ministry in the Church = Concilium* 64. New York: Herder & Herder, 1971.
A collection of articles by Catholics and non-Catholics on the papacy: need for reform, acceptability.

Lindbeck, George A. "Lutherans and the Papacy." *Journal of Ecumenical Studies* 13 (1976) 368–378.
A Lutheran theologian's proposal that his church develop a more positive attitude to the papacy.

McCord, Peter J., ed. *A Pope for All Christians?* New York: Paulist, 1976.
Collection of very important essays including that of Joseph Burgess, "Lutherans and the Papacy: A Review of Some Basic Issues" (17–47); Avery Dulles, "Papal Authority in Roman Catholicism" (48–70); J. Robert Wright, "Anglicans and the Papacy" (176–209).

Ohlig, Karl-Heinz. *Why We Need the Pope.* St. Meinrad: Abbey Press, 1975.
A radical Catholic presentation of the necessity and limits of papal primacy in an ecumenical perspective. Proposes that the papacy is not absolutely necessary to the Church.

de Satgé, John. *Peter and the Single Church.* London: SPCK, 1981.
An Anglican theologian argues that full obedience to the Gospel must include communion with the Pope.

Tavard, George H. "The Anglican-Roman Catholic Agreed Statements and their Reception." *Theological Studies* 41 (1980) 74–97.
Includes a section on the reception of the Venice Statement in which he outlines the positive and negative Anglican and Catholic reactions to the ARCIC report.

Yarnold, Edward J., and Chadwick, Henry. *Truth and Authority.* London: CTS/SPCK, 1977.
Two members of ARCIC provide this commentary on the Venice Statement which contains important background information and principles of interpretation.

The following books, selected from an extensive bibliography in French and German, are important sources for ecumenical discussion on the papacy outside the United States.

Allmen, Jean-Jacques von. *La primauté de Pierre et Paul: Remarques d'un protestant.* Cahiers oecuméniques 10. Fribough: Editions universitaires, 1977.

Arbeitsgemeinschaft ökumenischer Universitätsinstitute. *Papsttum als ökumenische Frage.* Munich: Kaiser, 1979; Mainz: Grünewald, 1979.

Brandenburg, Albert, and Urban, Hans Jörg, eds. *Petrus und Papst: Evangelium, Einheit der Kirche, Papstdienst.* Münster: Aschendorff, 1977.

Denzler, Georg, ed. *Das Papsttum in der Diskussion.* Regensburg: Pustet, 1974.

Denzler, Georg, ed. *Papsttum: heute und morgen.* Regensburg: Pustet, 1975.

Mund, Hans-Joachim, ed. *Das Petrusamt in der gegenwärtigen Diskussion.* Paderborn: Schöningh, 1976.

Mussner, Franz. *Petrus und Paulus: Pole der Einheit.* Quaestiones Disputatae 76. Freiburg: Herder, 1976.

Ratzinger, Joseph, ed. *Dienst an der Einheit: Zum Wesen und Auftrag des Petrusamts.* Düsseldorf: Patmos, 1978.

Scheffczyk, Leo. *Das unwandelbare im Petrusamt.* Berlin: Morus, 1971.

Stirnimann, Heinrich, and Vischer, Lukas. *Papsttum und Petrusdienst.* Ökumenische Perspektiven 7. Frankfurt: Lembeck und Knecht, 1975.

Thils, Gustave. *La primauté pontificale.* Recherches et Synthèses, Section de Dogme IV. Gembloux: Duculot, 1972.

Index of Names

Index of Subjects

Act of Supremacy (1534), 13
adiaphoron, 58, 60, 75
American Lutheran-Catholic
    Dialogue: necessity of the
    papacy, 61–63; origin of the
    papacy, 43–45; Petrine
    function 74–77, 80–81, 83;
    Petrine primacy, 23–24, 29
Anglican-Roman Catholic
    International Commission
    (ARCIC), 2, 26–30, 48–52,
    68–72, 82–84. *See also*
    Elucidation (1981); Final
    Report; Venice Statement;
    Windsor Statement
antichrist, Pope as: in Anglican
    theology, 13; in Lutheran
    theology, 12, 40–41
apostolic succession, 21, 50–51
ARCIC. *See* Anglican-Roman
    Catholic International
    Commission
Augsburg Confession, 59
Authority in the Church I (1976).
    See Venice Statement
Authority in the Church II (1981).
    See Windsor Statement

bene esse ecclesiae and the papacy:
    in Anglican theology, 63–67;
    in Lutheran theology, 58–59
Book of Concord (1580), 13

Canterbury, archbishop of: role in
    Anglican Communion, 46, 69
Caroline divines, 15–16, 24, 66
Chalcedon, Council of, 6–7
collegiality, 30, 55, 62, 68, 70
Congregation for the Doctrine of
    the Faith, 27, 30–31
Constantinople I, Council of, 14, 47
Councils. *See* Chalcedon,
    Constantinople I, Florence,
    Lyons II, Trent, Vatican I,
    Vatican II

*Differing Attitudes Toward Papal
    Primacy* (1974). *See* American
    Lutheran-Catholic Dialogue
divine design (*ordinatio divina*) of
    the papacy, 87–92
divine institution. *See* divine right
    of the papacy
divine right of the papacy: in
    American Lutheran-Catholic

Dialogue, 23–24, 44, 62; in
Anglican theology, 14, 45–48;
in Catholic theology, 9–10,
37–39, 87; as an ecumenical
problem, 2–3, 86–92; in Final
Report, 70–72; in Leo I, 6–7;
in Lutheran theology, 10–12,
41–42; meaning of
terminology, 9–10, 86–87; in
Middle Ages 7; at Vatican I, 9

ecumenical dialogues, official. *See*
American Lutheran-Catholic
Dialogue; Anglican-Roman
Catholic International
Commission; *Elucidation*
(1981); Final Report;
International Roman Catholic-
Lutheran Commission; Venice
Statement; Windsor Statement
Elucidation (1981), 26, 51, 69–70
English Litany (1544), 13
episcopacy: in Anglican theology,
64–65, 82; in Catholic
theology, 19, 78–79; in Final
Report, 27, 68; in Lutheran
theology, 76; at Vatican II, 21
episcope (oversight), 48, 51, 68–69,
72, 83
esse ecclesiae and the papacy: in
Anglican theology, 63, 66–67;
in Lutheran theology, 58–59
ex institutione divina. See divine
right of the papacy
ex ordinatione divina. See divine
design of the papacy

Final Report, 26–31, 48–52, 68–72,
83–84. *See also* Anglican-
Roman Catholic International

Commission; Venice
Statement; Windsor Statement
Florence, Council of, 7, 20
functionalists: need for the papacy,
54–56, 90; Petrine function/
primacy, 19–20, 77–78; Petrine
succession, 33–35

General Synod, Anglican (1977), 71

Holy Spirit, role in emergence of
the papacy: in American
Lutheran-Catholic Dialogue,
44–45; in Anglican theology,
48, 65, 89; in Catholic
theology, 35–36, 38–39, 55,
57, 88–89; in Final Report, 49,
51–52, 69; in Lutheran
theology, 42–43, 89
human right of the papacy: in
Anglican theology, 15, 90; in
Catholic theology, 19–20,
34–35, 90; in Lutheran
theology, 12–13, 40, 42–45, 90

infallibility, papal, 1, 17
International Roman Catholic-
Lutheran Commission, 81
irreversibility of the papacy: in
American Lutheran-Catholic
Dialogue, 63, 77; in Catholic
theology, 10, 33, 56–58

John 21:15–17, 8, 11, 20–21, 28.
See also Petrine texts

Lambeth Conferences, 64–65, 69,
82
Luke 22:31–32, 20, 28, 38. *See also*
Petrine texts
Lumen Gentium, 20–21

Commercial ~~…~~ ~~ries,~~ 1982. Softcover.

COMMERCIAL P~~A~~ ~~…~~ ~~(Text)~~
1988. Softcove ~~…w]~~

SPEIDEL'S BLACK LETTER ON
SALES AND SALES FINANCING,
363 pages, 1984. Softcover.
(Review)

STOCKTON'S SALES IN A NUT-
SHELL, Second Edition, 370
pages, 1981. Softcover.
(Text)

STONE'S UNIFORM COMMERCIAL
CODE IN A NUTSHELL, Third
Edition, 580 pages, 1989.
Softcover. (Text)

WEBER AND SPEIDEL'S COMMER-
CIAL PAPER IN A NUTSHELL,
Third Edition, 404 pages,
1982. Softcover. (Text)

WHITE AND SUMMERS' HORN-
BOOK ON THE UNIFORM COM-
MERCIAL CODE, Third Edition,
Student Edition, 1386 pages,
1988. (Text)

Community Property

MENNELL AND BOYKOFF'S COM-
MUNITY PROPERTY IN A NUT-
SHELL, Second Edition, 432
pages, 1988. Softcover.
(Text)

Comparative Law

GLENDON, GORDON AND
OSAKWE'S COMPARATIVE LEGAL
TRADITIONS IN A NUTSHELL.

Conflict of Laws

HAY'S BLACK LETTER ON CON-
FLICT OF LAWS, 330 pages,
1989. Softcover. (Review)

SCOLES AND HAY'S HORNBOOK
ON CONFLICT OF LAWS, Student
Edition, 1085 pages, 1982,
with 1988–89 pocket part.
(Text)

SEIGEL'S CONFLICTS IN A NUT-
SHELL, 470 pages, 1982. Softcover. (Text)

Constitutional Law—Civil Rights

BARRON AND DIENES' BLACK
LETTER ON CONSTITUTIONAL
LAW, Second Edition, 310
pages, 1987. Softcover. (Review)

BARRON AND DIENES' CONSTITU-
TIONAL LAW IN A NUTSHELL,
389 pages, 1986. Softcover.
(Text)

ENGDAHL'S CONSTITUTIONAL
FEDERALISM IN A NUTSHELL,
Second Edition, 411 pages,
1987. Softcover. (Text)

MARKS AND COOPER'S STATE
CONSTITUTIONAL LAW IN A NUT-
SHELL, 329 pages, 1988. Soft-
cover. (Text)

NOWAK, ROTUNDA AND

Constitutional Law—Civil Rights—Continued

YOUNG'S HORNBOOK ON CONSTITUTIONAL LAW, Third Edition, 1191 pages, 1986 with 1988 pocket part. (Text)

VIEIRA'S CONSTITUTIONAL CIVIL RIGHTS IN A NUTSHELL, Second Edition, approximately 320 pages, 1990. Softcover. (Text)

WILLIAMS' CONSTITUTIONAL ANALYSIS IN A NUTSHELL, 388 pages, 1979. Softcover. (Text)

Consumer Law—see also Commercial Law

EPSTEIN AND NICKLES' CONSUMER LAW IN A NUTSHELL, Second Edition, 418 pages, 1981. Softcover. (Text)

Contracts

CALAMARI, AND PERILLO'S BLACK LETTER ON CONTRACTS, 397 pages, 1983. Softcover. (Review)

CALAMARI AND PERILLO'S HORNBOOK ON CONTRACTS, Third Edition, 1049 pages, 1987. (Text)

CORBIN'S TEXT ON CONTRACTS, One Volume Student Edition, 1224 pages, 1952. (Text)

FRIEDMAN'S CONTRACT REME-
DIES IN A NUTSHELL, 323 pages, 1981. Softcover. (Text)

KEYES' GOVERNMENT CONTRACTS IN A NUTSHELL, 423 pages, 1979. Softcover. (Text)

SCHABER AND ROHWER'S CONTRACTS IN A NUTSHELL, Second Edition, 425 pages, 1984. Softcover. (Text)

Copyright—see Patent and Copyright Law

Corporations

HAMILTON'S BLACK LETTER ON CORPORATIONS, Second Edition, 513 pages, 1986. Softcover. (Review)

HAMILTON'S THE LAW OF CORPORATIONS IN A NUTSHELL, Second Edition, 515 pages, 1987. Softcover. (Text)

HENN AND ALEXANDER'S HORNBOOK ON LAWS OF CORPORATIONS, Third Edition, Student Edition, 1371 pages, 1983, with 1986 pocket part. (Text)

Corrections

KRANTZ' THE LAW OF CORRECTIONS AND PRISONERS' RIGHTS IN A NUTSHELL, Third Edition, 407 pages, 1988. Softcover. (Text)

POPPER'S POST-CONVICTION REMEDIES IN A NUTSHELL, 360